An Educational Masterpiece!

Not since Harry Wong's seminal work, **The First Days of School***, has there been a more important book at a more crucial time. Reading and applying Hal Urban's strategies will enable any teacher, with practice and effort, to reach performance excellence in his or her craft. But more important,* **Lessons from the Classroom: 20 Things Good Teachers Do** *will rekindle or ignite your passion for the noblest occupation of humanity — the education of our youth.*

For years people who have heard Hal speak at conferences have been saying, "I wish everyone on my staff could get his message." Well, your wish has now been granted. Within these pages Hal shares the insight and wisdom that guided his 35 years of classroom excellence. I can think of no book that I would recommended more highly to an experienced or novice educator. It is simply the best one I've ever read for the teacher who wants to perform at the highest level, and help his or her students do the same.

This is an educational masterpiece!

Dr. Phil Vincent

Author, **Restoring School Civility**

A portion of the profit from each book sold will be donated to
The Center for the 4th & 5th R's
(Respect & Responsibility)
Cortland, New York

Ordering instructions can be found on the last page - 252

Brilliant, Simple, Practical!

This is just plain wonderful. It's a one-of-a-kind teaching manual that shows us some of the important things teachers can do to make a difference in their students' lives. It's full of brilliant, yet simple and practical ways to connect with kids and help them develop in an atmosphere that fosters mutual respect, hard work, and a love of learning.

Hal covers all the essentials that have been set aside due to the "No Child Left Untested" mania. An award-winning teacher, he reminds us often that we can maintain high standards in both academics and character, and have fun in the process. His love for teaching and for his students comes through on every page.

I absolutely love this book! I hope every teacher in the country reads it and applies these valuable lessons.

Dr. Michele Borba

*Author, **Building Moral Intelligence***

LESSONS FROM THE CLASSROOM

20 Things Good Teachers Do

HAL URBAN

Great Lessons Press

Great Lessons Press

For information about special discounts on bulk purchases,
please contact Great Lessons Press:

650/366-0882 or halurban@halurban.com

Cover design and interior layout by
MacGraphics Services
Aurora, Colorado
www.MacGraphics.net

Printed in the United States of America by
McNaughton & Gunn, Inc.
Saline, Michigan
www.bookprinters.com

ISBN13 – 978-0-9659684-1-6

ISBN – 0-9659684-1-3

Dedicated to a great teacher, colleague, and friend

Marvin Berkowitz

Thank you for the inspiration and encouragement to write this book

Who dares to teach must never cease to learn.

– John Cotton Dana

Lessons From The Classroom
20 Things Good Teachers Do

Table of Contents

One simple reason for writing this book

A teacher affects eternity; he can never tell where
his influence stops.

— Henry Adams

I was a classroom teacher in a public school for 35 years. My tour of duty ran from September 1966 to June 2001. I've been in recovery ever since. It's been going exceedingly well, and my sanity is still intact — although some might argue otherwise. What's been most helpful in the process has been the opportunity to frequently share my experiences with other teachers. I'm not sure if this qualifies as group therapy or not, but I've loved every minute of it.

In 1995, I started receiving invitations to speak to teachers in various schools around the country because the simple message about old-fashioned virtues contained in my first book, *Life's Greatest Lessons*, seemed to strike a chord. I talk to them about developing good character traits in our young people while maintaining high academic standards, and about the most effective teaching strategies I learned during those many years in the classroom. Speaking to teachers has been almost as much fun as was teaching itself, and it's considerably easier. I've met thousands of wonderful educators from all over the world, and I've enjoyed sharing my experiences with them. All of this has further contributed to my recovery, mental health, and happiness. I've been richly blessed.

While my survival and continuing sanity are noteworthy, they have nothing to do with why I wrote this book. I wrote it because hundreds of those teachers in my audiences have encouraged me to put my teaching philosophy and strategies in writing. Well, here they are. My sole reason for doing this is to leave something of value behind for my friends and colleagues in the teaching profession. I had an indescribably enjoyable and rewarding career, learned hundreds of valuable things about what works in teaching (and quite a few that don't), and want to pass on some of the best of them to the present and future generations of educators. You hold the most important jobs in the world.

I touch the future. I teach.

– Christa McAuliffe, 1948-1986
Teacher and astronaut

The author's sources

It's important to note at the beginning that all the ideas and suggestions presented here didn't come from the creative genius of Hal Urban. In fact, I'm pretty sure that I don't have any creative genius. But I do have 35 years of classroom experiences. Those experiences, along with what I learned by reading, observing, talking to other teachers, listening to my students, and attending conferences, taught me valuable lessons about what good teachers do. These are the main sources of what you'll read here. I used them, along with trial-and-error, to figure out how to become one of those good teachers.

I wasn't the best teacher at either of the two schools in which I taught, but I *was* the best teacher I could be. The most important thing was that I wanted to get better every year, and I think I did. I live by two personal mottos and brought both to school every day. The first one: "Always give your best." It's a motto for me for the simple reason that I had two great role models while growing up. My father was an ironworker and my mother managed the household. There was never a day in which both of them didn't conscientiously give the best they had to those two important roles. They passed on a legacy of hard work that I always wanted to live up to. And in June 2001, when I walked out of my classroom for the last time, a wonderful feeling came over me. It was the satisfaction of knowing that I'd always given my best.

My other motto: "Celebrate today!" It means that each new day is full of good things, good people, and countless opportunities. I never wanted to miss any of them, and I didn't want my students to miss them, either. That's why at the beginning of every class I asked them, "What are we celebrating today?" This was the philosophy and attitude with which I approached my classroom each day. I always expected good things to happen.

> *We often find that life responds to our outlook. What*
> *we expect to happen, happens. The dreams we choose*
> *to believe in come to be.*

> *– Wynn Davis*

Some important clarifications

As much as I would like it to be, this book isn't a cure-all for everything that ails education. And as much as I would like it to, it doesn't have the power of a magic wand to turn you into the world's greatest teacher and make all your students perfectly polite and eager to learn. If I claimed these things, we'd have to place the book in the fiction section, more specifically under the "Fantasy" heading. And they'd have to place me in an institution to get help with my delusions.

The book is intended to be a resource and a guide, not a mandate. I hope you'll find suggestions here that are rooted in common sense, are practical, and are simple to apply in your particular setting. The strategies here are time-honored. They've been around a long time and have been passed down from the great teachers who came before us. But please be aware of the following realities:

1 – No teacher (including this one) has all the answers

Although I taught for 35 years, I make no claim to having all the world's knowledge about our profession. No one does, and no one ever will. I was still learning in my last year in the classroom, and I'd no doubt still be learning if I'd remained there. I'm simply sharing here what I found to be most valuable during my tour of duty. There are no guarantees that everything presented here will work the same for you as it did for me, but I obviously hope it does.

2 – No strategy works every time

I'm confident that most of the philosophies and strategies in this book will work *most* of the time, but that's not the same as claiming they'll work *all* of the time. Researchers frequently remind us that "variables" can profoundly affect a study. Variables also can affect one's teaching success. Among them are your personality, your work ethic, the culture of the school, the types of students you have, parent values and involvement, and the standards of the community in which you teach. My suggestion is that you take all of these into account, be realistic in your expectations, and simply do all that you can to be the best teacher possible.

3 – Don't expect to reach every student

I frequently receive e-mails from teachers which start like this: "I have this student who ..." They describe a kid with a bad attitude, obnoxious behavior, and a poor work ethic. Then they ask, "What should I do?" They're looking for the magic wand that I don't have. There is no one-solution-fits-all for problem students. I don't have answers for these types of questions, unfortunately, because I don't know enough about the teacher, the student, or the setting. And most important, I remind these teachers who contact me that I wasn't able to reach every one of the 9,000-plus students I taught. I tried, but occasionally I had to remind myself that even Ted Williams struck out once in a while.

Some kids come to us scarred by life at an early age, some come to us with emotional problems, and some come to us unready to learn. My suggestion is to treat each case individually, do everything within your power to help the student, and make a decision based on what's best for the student, your class, and you. The simple truth is that you can't win them all. And you shouldn't beat yourself up if you can't. If you can succeed with 90 to 95 percent of your students, you're an awesome teacher.

4 – These are suggestions, not rules

Please understand that I'm sharing ideas with you here. I'm sprinkling out a lot of suggestions that you should feel free to accept, reject, or tweak to fit your own needs. Maybe instead of doing exactly what I did, you'll get an idea, modify it, and come up with a similar strategy that works for you. There is no one perfect plan that works for every teacher in exactly the same way. But there are some general principles of good teaching. My goal is to share them with you and allow you to work out the details.

5 – The most important variable is the personality of the teacher

We're all born with a different set of genes, and we've all had different experiences. The result is that we all end up with vastly different personalities. In other words, we have vastly different ways of presenting ourselves to the world, which includes our students. I didn't try to act like William Glasser or Marva Collins, but I *did* learn valuable philosophies and strategies from them. It's important that you be yourself. But keep in mind that your personality isn't a strait jacket. It doesn't have to hold you back. And as I always told my students, "You can never grow unless you're willing to take some steps outside your comfort zone."

Let me give you an example based on my own career. By nature, I'm a very introverted person. I spend a lot of time alone and I'm pretty quiet – some might even say boring – at social gatherings. But when I teach or speak, it's a completely different story. I decided long ago that I wouldn't be able to reach out to my students if I always stayed within my comfort zone. I challenged myself, took steps out of it, and I was able to connect with my students much more effectively as a result. I wasn't being phony; I was simply playing the leadership role that would be most effective in my profession. People in all walks of life do it successfully every day.

6 – Most of these strategies work at all grade levels

Although I was a full-time high school teacher and a part-time university professor, I've learned that most of the strategies I used work with students at any grade level. Since 1995 I've visited hundreds of elementary and middle schools, have talked to kids of all ages, and have spoken to thousands of teachers. The children continually prove that a positive attitude, good manners, hard work, kind words, honesty, setting goals, and making good choices work for people of all ages. And their teachers assure me that almost all of the strategies I share with them work in their classrooms as well.

This makes perfect sense for two reasons. First, I picked up a lot of creative ideas from elementary and middle school teachers while attending conferences all over the country. I took their ideas home with me, tweaked some of them and used them in my high school classes. They worked. Second, I learned something valuable about teenagers early in my career. On some days they can be perfectly mature young adults, and on others they can act like third-graders. No wonder most of these strategies work with kids of all ages.

In 2004, I received a wonderful e-mail from a third-grade teacher in New Hampshire. She'd attended a summer conference at which I'd conducted an all-day workshop on many of my teaching strategies. She wrote, "Thank you for sharing your hard-earned wisdom with us. I starting putting many of them to use on the first day of school, and you're right – they *do* work with kids of all ages. The most amazing thing is that they're so simple. I'm having more fun than ever. So are my students." A week later I received a packet of letters from the third-graders in her class. One little boy wrote, "Dear Dr. Urban, Your conference in New York must have been really great. I don't know what you did with Ms. Genet, but she sure came back in a good mood."

The first two weeks of school

What you do on the first days of school will determine your success or failure for the rest of the school year. You will either win or lose your class on the first days of school.

– Harry Wong and Rosemary Wong
The First Days of School

I don't think there's ever been a statement about teaching with which I agree more strongly than the one above by my friends and colleagues Harry and Rosemary Wong. The longer I was in the classroom, the more I was convinced that what I did in the first two weeks of school was critically important. I compare what a teacher does during the first weeks of school to what a contractor does when he builds a home. He lays a solid foundation first. No matter how nice the home might look, it will crumble if it isn't set on a solid foundation. Both the teacher and the students need that same solid foundation, and the laying of it must begin on the first day of school.

Most of what I suggest here can be established in the first two weeks. I guarantee that if a teacher does these effectively in the first 10 to 15 days of school, the rest of the year will go more smoothly. The students will behave better, work harder, and perform at a higher academic level. This may seem like a brash statement, but I put in enough years to know that it's true. I gave up some academic time early in the school year in order to create an environment in which I could teach and my students could learn. Any academic time we "lost" in those first few weeks were made up a hundred-fold in the remaining months.

I've had teachers tell me, "I don't have time to do those things. I've got to get right at it. We're under a lot of pressure to raise test scores." I know the feeling because the testing madness started about five years before I left the classroom. But I still contend that if a teacher establishes the right atmosphere and the right procedures in the first few weeks of the school year, he or she will have more time during the rest of the year to devote to academics. As Harry and Rosemary Wong remind us, teachers win or lose their classes in the first days of school. If you win over your classes, everything else falls into place. And yes, even test scores will go up.

A nuts and bolts approach

Several years ago a dear friend and colleague told me, "What I like most about you is that you're a nuts-and-bolts kind of guy." At first I thought he was telling me that I was nuts, but then I realized that he was giving me a compliment. I had an inkling of what he meant, but I asked him to explain. He said, "You always seem to be able to cut through the crap and get right to the point. I find that refreshing." I hope his description of me also describes what I tried to do while writing this book.

I've done my best to avoid explaining profound theories, using educational jargon, spouting ivory-tower intellectual concepts, and using polysyllabic words that will drive you to the dictionary. Be thankful that I'm not smart enough to do any of those things. My dominant personality traits seem to be logic and common sense. These can be good or bad, depending upon circumstances, but I think they served me well in both teaching and writing – at least that's what my students and readers have told me. They seem to appreciate, as my friend did, that I get right to the point. I've tried to do that here.

I've also tried to avoid filling pages with fluff. I've seen in it too many books about teaching, and I always find it a little syrupy and sometimes insulting. You will, however, find a lot of stories here. I could have written a much shorter book by leaving them out, but I've always believed that a teacher, a speaker, or a writer makes his points clearer and more personal with a good story. Thus, I couldn't resist telling some of mine. I hope they add meaning and enjoyment to your reading.

Stories are how we learn.

– Bill Mooney, David Holt
The Storyteller's Guide

The challenge and rewards of teaching

Most of all, I hope my philosophies, stories, and strategies help you and your colleagues to better meet the incredible daily challenge we face in providing an education for our children, teenagers, and young adults. I hope you bring out the best in them, and I hope you find some practical tools here that help. Teaching is probably more challenging now than it's ever been. At the same time, it has the potential to be more rewarding than it's ever been.

Teachers can change lives with just the right mix
of chalk and challenges.

– Joyce A. Myers

I can't imagine a profession that is more
challenging, stimulating, or rewarding.

– Peter J. Horn

Good teachers share one special quality

Good teaching is as much about passion as it is about reason ... It's about caring for your craft, having a passion for it, and conveying that passion to everyone, most importantly to your students.

*– Professor Richard Leblanc
Award-winning teacher,
York University, Ontario*

Who were your favorite teachers?

If I asked you to name your favorite teachers from kindergarten through graduate school, it would be easy to answer, wouldn't it? It would also be an enjoyable question to answer because it would bring back so many fond memories of wonderful people who've touched both your personal life and your professional life. You would be thinking about people who not only taught you things of value, but also inspired you. Quite possibly, they inspired you to become a teacher.

Many years ago, my classmates and I were asked this question on my first day in the teaching credential program at the University of San Francisco. It was a great way to begin my pursuit of a career in teaching – thinking about people in the profession who had the most positive influence on me. We were asked to write down our answers. I thought of Sister Mary Margaret and Sister Mary

Anne, who taught me in elementary school. I thought of Mrs. Padgett and Mrs. Kofford, both English teachers, and Mr. Kutras, a history teacher, in high school. Then I thought of Dr. Lincoln and Dr. Campbell, history professors, and Dr. Kirk, an English professor, from my college days. Then came this question: "What do they all have in common?" My hand went up first, and Dr. McSweeney, another great teacher, called on me. I said, "They all *loved* what they were doing. They had great enthusiasm for teaching." All of my fellow graduate students nodded their heads in agreement. One of them, to punctuate the point, said, "Exactly!"

That was apparently the answer Dr. McSweeney expected. He said, "I ask that question every year, and I always get the same answer." He went on to explain that he opens with that question because it's guaranteed to get things off to a good start, and it gets future teachers to think about what separates the great teachers from the not-so-great. He said, "We all remember our favorite teachers – the ones who had passion and enthusiasm, the ones who loved and enjoyed what they were doing. We want each of you to become that kind of teacher. Always remember those special teachers. Make your career a tribute to them." It's a statement I never once forgot during my 35 years in the classroom.

Having fun while working hard

There are other words that are similar to enthusiasm and passion. They also apply to our favorite teachers. Here are a few of them:

zest	excitement	energy	fervor
eagerness	enjoyment	delight	zeal
liveliness	vitality	vigor	devotion

There's yet another important word that goes with all of the above in describing the best teachers: FUN! Good teachers, along with working very hard, almost always have fun. Have you ever noticed how much they smile while they're teaching? One of my greatest colleagues once said, "I don't know of any other job I could do and have this much fun. Just think, I get paid for coming here every day and having fun." Like most teachers, he didn't get paid nearly enough for what he did, but the other rewards that come from good teaching more than made up for it.

Fun is important because it's usually a two-way street. If the teacher's having fun, there's a good chance the students are, too. Students of all ages appreciate a teacher who's having a good time. And make no mistake: Hard work and dedication do not impede you from having fun. In fact, one of the valuable things I learned during my student teaching was that the harder I worked *outside* of class, particularly in terms of preparation, the more fun I had *inside* the class. When students say that a teacher is "fun" or teaches a "fun class," they don't mean that teacher is all about fun and games, or that the class isn't about teaching and learning. They simply mean that the teacher enjoys what he or she is doing, and that it becomes an important part of the atmosphere of the classroom. In the teaching profession, hard work and fun go together.

I'm not claiming that every day in the classroom is going to be all rainbows and smiles and shiny red apples just because you come in fired up with enthusiasm. But I *am* saying that you increase the odds of teaching effectively and having cooperative students every time you do bring that passion. People in all professions have their bad days; CEOs blow deals, plumbers break pipes, and running backs fumble at the goal line. Having a bad day once in a while is part of life. We've all had our share of disappointments. But a passion for what you're doing can help keep those days at a minimum.

> *Enthusiasm releases the drive to*
> *carry you over obstacles and adds*
> *significance to all you do.*
>
> – Norman Vincent Peale

Enthusiasm spelled out

Near the end of my career as a classroom teacher, I was asked to speak to a group of graduate students in education at Santa Clara University. All of them were working toward their California teaching credential. Some were taking the beginning courses in the program, while others were doing their student teaching. I told them I was happy to be there because they had three wonderful qualities: youth, idealism, and enthusiasm. I told them the key to having a successful and rewarding teaching career would be in maintaining all three. I said, "No matter how old you get, you can still maintain your youthful spirit. If you can do this, you should also be able to maintain your idealism and your enthusiasm."

I asked them if they'd met any burned-out and cynical teachers yet. They all assured me they had. I asked them if they'd heard comments like this (cue nasty tone of voice): "Oh, yeah, you're young and idealistic now, but just wait until you've been teaching as long as I have. Then we'll see how excited you are." Again, I was told by the aspiring educators that they'd heard comments like these often. So I did everything I could to assure them that it doesn't have to be that way. I never lost an ounce of enthusiasm for teaching, even in my 35th year, and I had many outstanding colleagues who felt the same way. It was their continued enthusiasm for teaching that made them so successful year after year.

While preparing for the Santa Clara presentation, I started playing around with each of the 10 letters in the word enthusiasm, and I had a lot of fun coming up with other words that paint a picture of what successful teachers do. The graduate students loved it. One of them, skilled in computer graphics, made a small ENTHUSIASM! poster, which included all the words. She printed out one for each of her classmates and sent a copy to me. Here are the other words:

Energetic – Let's face it. Teaching is a high-energy job. The lifeless need not apply. The students we spend the day with have energy to spare, and we need to be able to keep up with them. Stay in shape and take your vitamins.

Not boring – Here are the four most frequent complaints I heard from students about teachers:

1 – "He has no control over the class."

2 – "I'm not learning anything from her."

3 – "He's so mean."

4 – "She's so boring."

I'll address the issues of control, learning, and being mean in other chapters of this book. Let me address the boring issue here. Simply put, it's impossible to be boring and excited at the same time. If you're genuinely excited about what you're doing, there won't be any complaints about being boring.

Tough – Teaching is not a job for sissies. We have to be physically and mentally tough because the job is so demanding. There also are times when we need to be tough on the kids. Not mean, but tough. We need to let them know that we're not afraid to make them work. We need to hold them accountable, and they need to know that we will.

High standards – Good teachers consistently maintain high standards in two important areas. The first is classroom management – establishing a culture that's conducive to teaching and learning, one that's built on a foundation of mutual respect. The other is academics – letting students and their parents know that we take seriously the responsibility of helping the next generation acquire the knowledge they'll need to function well in society.

Understanding – By this I mean understanding what's going on in our students' lives – developing empathy for them. It's a lot harder being a kid now than it was when we were growing up, and we need to acknowledge this. We should make every effort possible to learn what's going on in their lives, what affects their learning. It's also important for us to remember our own days as students. What was it like on a bad day? When were we distracted? When were we at our best? How did our best teachers treat us in both good and bad times?

Sense of humor – You will die in the classroom without one. An important aspect of enthusiasm for teaching – and for life – is the ability to see and enjoy the funny things that surround us daily. While everyone likes to laugh, it's been proven that kids laugh about 10 times more than the average adult. Teachers, more than anyone, need to understand this. Laughter makes every classroom a better place. This doesn't mean that you have to be Robin Williams every day. It just means that you should never miss an opportunity to laugh with your kids and at yourself. Laughter is the shortest distance between people of all ages.

Imagination – Albert Einstein said imagination is more important than intellect. Most certainly, this applies to the teaching profession. You could have a Ph.D. from Harvard and be a renowned expert in your subject area, but if you can't present your material creatively you'll bomb. Keep in mind that good teaching is an art. It requires some degree of imagination and resourcefulness. Always look for new and better ways of making your material interesting. It will be more enjoyable for you and your students.

Always prepared – Someone once asked me what the most demanding and time-consuming part of teaching was. Without a second's hesitation, I answered in one word: PREPARATION! Nothing is more important to a teacher. It would have absolutely terrified me to walk into a classroom without being fully prepared. In fact, I usually suggest that teachers be over-prepared. At the same time, we need to be flexible. Good teachers are able to capitalize on serendipitous moments when they occur, no matter how solid their lesson plans are.

Storyteller – In my first year of teaching, one of the best teachers at my school gave me some advice that was invaluable, and I've been passing it on for more than 40 years. He said, "If you want to make a point with your students, put it into a story. They'll tune out a lecture, but they'll always listen to a good story."

All good teachers – along with good preachers, speakers, and writers – are good storytellers. Everyone loves a good story.

Motivated – "Real motivation comes from within." That's the title of Chapter 11 in my first book, *Life's Greatest Lessons*. Good teachers understand this. They keep an inner fire burning rather than wait for someone else to light one for them. In addition, they help their students become motivated. This happens because good teachers are also good salespeople – they sell ideas. They help their students understand why it's so important to pass on knowledge, and they help them see education not as an obligation, but as an opportunity to improve the quality of their lives.

Two types of teacher enthusiasm

If you took a survey among the best teachers you know and asked them what they enjoy the most about their jobs, a large percentage of them would give you two answers. I know this because I conducted such a survey during the years 2006-2007. While attending conferences and visiting schools throughout the country, I informally interviewed more than 200 teachers at all grade levels. Among the many questions I asked, these were the most important ones: "Why are you so enthusiastic about your job? What do you like most about teaching?" Almost all of them gave me the same two answers.

1 – Enthusiasm for the kids

Good teachers love their students. They may not love every kid at every moment, but in general, they enjoy being with young people who are full of energy and always on the edge of discovery. These teachers have a special knack for connecting with them, for helping them open their minds.

If you do any reading about the history and philosophy of education, you'll find that great teachers of the past all agree that learning is usually the result of a good relationship between the teacher and the student. Good teaching is personal. This was pointed out during one of my first graduate seminars in a course called Philosophy of Education. Our professor, Dr. Tom McSweeney, shared with us two of his favorite old sayings about the relationship between teachers and students. He claimed then, as I do now, that they capture the essence of effective teaching:

"Kids don't care how much you know until they know how much you care."

You could have a bachelor's degree from Yale, a master's degree from Stanford, and a doctorate from M.I.T. You could have written a scholarly book that won the Pulitzer Prize. You could be considered the world's foremost authority in nuclear technology. The kids couldn't care less. All they want to know is: Can you connect with them? Do you understand them? Do you really care about them? And no matter what ages they are, they'll know the answers to all of these questions after spending only a few days with you in class. Teachers are public servants. Let your students know – and show them – how much you care.

"If you can reach 'em, you can teach 'em."

Our students are no different than we are when it comes to wanting a basic human need met. They want to feel as though they count. They don't want to be regarded by the teacher as students who sit in particular desks. They want to be regarded as human beings whose lives and feelings and aspirations are important. One of the greatest educators who ever lived crystallized this thought back in the early 1900s:

> *The deepest urge in human nature is the desire to feel important.*
> *– John Dewey*

Dewey doesn't say they want to feel more important than everyone else. They just want to feel as if they count. There are many ways in which teachers can fill this need that all students have. I'll be discussing some of them throughout this book, especially in chapters four and six.

2 – Enthusiasm for teaching

Among teacher variables, enthusiasm has the most powerful and positive impact on student learning.
> – *Toni Kempler*

If you ask 100 great teachers what their most important professional quality is, almost all of them will answer "dedication," "passion," "zeal," "enthusiasm," or "love of teaching." They won't talk about their degrees or how much they know. They'll talk about how genuinely excited they are about their jobs. If you ask 100 people who aren't even in the field of education what the most important quality of a good teacher is, they'll give you answers that are almost identical to those of the teachers. They remember their best teachers as the ones who loved their jobs.

In other words, we all seem to have this "gut" feeling that when it comes to good teaching, enthusiasm is the key element. But we need to remember that within the field of education there's an important group of people who keep us honest and on our toes by constantly asking these kinds of questions: Has it been researched? Do the findings support your theory? I'm happy to answer YES – teacher enthusiasm has been researched. And I'm even happier to answer YES – the findings do support our theory.

Toni Kempler, quoted above, earned her PhD in Education and Psychology at the University of Michigan in Ann Arbor. As I write this, she's a Professor of Education at Rutgers University, and she's one of those important people referred to above who conducts meticulous research in the interest of good teaching. She and two of her colleagues conducted a study in which they set out to measure the importance of teacher enthusiasm. Their results were published in *The Journal of Experimental Education*, spring, 2000. The title of their article is, "What's Everybody So Excited About? : The Effects of Teacher Enthusiasm on Student Intrinsic Motivation and Vitality."

Through the miracle we call the Internet, I found more than 40 other studies, conducted within the past 10 years, on teacher enthusiasm. The research involved teachers and students at all grade levels, from elementary school to graduate school. It was conducted through experiments, surveys, observation, case studies, and interviews. The results were remarkably similar. Research does bear out that enthusiasm is a special quality that all great teachers share.

> *It is important that teachers be able to communicate a sense of excitement about the subjects they teach.*
> *—David Ausubel*
> *Educational psychologist*

> *Not only does teacher enthusiasm help make a course more enjoyable and entertaining for students and the teacher, it has also been shown to help the learner retain larger amounts of information.*
> *—W. D. Coats*
> *Educational psychologist*

> *Enthusiasm is the mother of effort, and without it nothing great was ever achieved.*
>
> *—Ralph Waldo Emerson*

> *If you love what you are doing you will be successful.*
> *—Albert Schweitzer*

Good teachers have two important goals

*To educate a person in mind and not in morals
is to educate a menace to society.*

–Theodore Roosevelt

*Intelligence is not enough. Intelligence plus
character – that is the true goal of education.*

–Martin Luther King, Jr.

Educating the whole person

The two most valuable courses I took during teacher training were History of Education and Philosophy of Education. I had a bachelor's and a master's degree in history, and had a great love for the subject. It was valuable to learn the origins of the profession I was entering. And since I was Jesuit-trained with an undergraduate minor in philosophy, I also appreciated learning that aspect of teaching. As you might suspect, there was quite a bit of overlap in the two courses. It's impossible to teach the history of anything without including theories of the great thinkers of the era.

What I remember most about these two courses was the time devoted to two of the most influential philosophers in history: Confucius and Aristotle. Although one came from ancient China and the other from ancient Greece, they were remarkably similar in their beliefs about what constituted a good education. From an academic perspective, they felt strongly that each generation had an obligation to pass on its accumulated knowledge to the next. But both were equally adamant that morals and virtuous living also should be taught to youth.

Confucius (551-479 BC) emphasized helping young people cultivate character, purity of heart, and right conduct. Aristotle (384-322 BC) told us that the aim of education is "to make men both smart and good." We make them good, he said, when we help them develop moral virtue.

Horace Mann (1796-1859) is often called "The Father of American Education," as he contributed more to the development of public schools in this country than any other person. Mann agreed with Confucius and Aristotle that the two primary goals of education are to increase knowledge and to develop good citizens. He said that it was important for children to learn to read, write, and spell, and to learn math, science, geography, and history. But he said it was even more important to build good character. Like President Thomas Jefferson, Mann believed that training in good character would produce responsible and virtuous citizens who would make the new republic flourish. Mann often quoted from the wisdom of Solomon, and he was particularly fond of saying, "Train up a child in the way he should go; and when he is old he will not depart from it." (Proverbs 22:6 NIV)

And so it went throughout history. Increasing knowledge and developing good character formed a dual foundation of our educational system. When I started school way back in the late 1940s, it was made clear to us on the first day that we were there for the same two reasons everyone goes to school: to learn academic subjects and to become good citizens. We were even told that we would be graded in both areas. My first report card was about the size of two postcards, side by side. It looked something like this:

Citizenship	Academics
___ Respect for authority	___ Reading
___ Respect for peers	___ Writing
___ Respect for property	___ Mathematics
___ Work ethic	___ Social Studies
___ Honesty	___ Art

Although the list of topics above isn't complete, it does give you an idea of how serious schools were about blending academics with character building. We were given letter grades on both sides of the card. My parents would accept a B+ in one of my academic subjects, but there would have to be a lot of explaining if I got anything less than an A in the citizenship grades. Knowing we were getting graded in those areas kept us on our toes and on our best behavior. Looking back, I realize this kind of accountability was valuable for us. And I can't help wishing that more schools and teachers were holding students accountable for their behavior today. The ones that do, the ones with successful character education programs, are enjoying respectful student behavior *and* academic improvement. They go together.

The disappearance and re-emergence of character education

Ironically, the character development aspect of education began to fade out just as I began my teaching career in the mid to late 1960s. There were a number of converging social changes, many full of turmoil, which contributed to it: the civil rights movement, the college protests, the women's liberation movement, the war in Vietnam, the decline in influence of religion, the weakening of the family, growing materialism accompanied by slick new advertising strategies, an increasingly powerful (and often sleazy) media, and the emergence of moral relativism. Character development took a back seat during the 60s, 70s, and 80s, a period in which we needed it more than ever. The increase in self-centeredness and the decline in civility during those years were truly alarming. They had a major impact on our children.

> *There is today a widespread, deeply unsettling sense that children are changing – in ways that tell us much about ourselves as a society. And these changes are reflected not just in the violent extremes of teenage behavior but in the everyday speech and actions of younger children as well.*
>
> – *Dr. Thomas Lickona*

Here's the good news: Character education started its comeback in the early 1990s. In July of 1992, Michael Josephson of the Josephson Institute of Ethics invited more than 30 educational leaders to a meeting in Aspen, Colorado. The people who attended represented state school boards, teachers' unions, universities, ethics centers, youth organizations, and religious groups. The result was the Aspen Declaration On Character Education. It includes eight principles, or reasons, as to why character education is so critical. They're summed up in the last one:

> *The character and conduct of our youth reflect*
> *the character and conduct of society; therefore,*
> *every adult has the responsibility to teach and*
> *model the core ethical values and every social*
> *institution has the responsibility to promote the*
> *development of good character.*

This was the first step in the revival of character education. Michael Josephson founded Character Counts!; Tom Lickona started The Center for the 4th & 5th R's (respect & responsibility); and the Character Education Partnership was launched in 1993. CEP is a national coalition of leaders committed to putting character education back into our schools. It includes people in government, schools and colleges, business, labor, places of worship, and service organizations.

In addition, a number of organizations began to sponsor character education conferences. There are now state, regional, and national conferences held throughout the year. (See the appendix for a list of organizations and conferences.) While there's still much to be done, the progress made in character education between the Aspen meeting in 1992 and the writing of this book in 2007 has been truly phenomenal.

If character education is a new concept for you, I suggest you look in the appendix, not only for the names of organizations and conferences, but for books as well. Even simpler, do what everyone does when they need to know something: "Google" character education. You'll find the answers to every question you have.

Because the comeback of character education has been going on since the early 1990s, and because there's so much material available, I don't see a need to explain it in great detail here. However, there are a few basic issues that I'd like to address.

Four obstacles to character education – and a response to each

Obstacle #1 – "Whose values are you going to teach?"

This was a common – and legitimate – question asked back in the early 90s. It's still occasionally asked today. Because we have a wide variety of cultures and belief systems within our country, many parents have a valid concern about the values that are taught to their children.

Response – The values that we all share.

To begin with, I prefer the word *virtues* to the word *values*. Virtues refer to behavior that's honorable and good. Values refer to the principles we consider to be important.

Regardless of which word we use, there *are* values that are shared by the world community. This includes people of all races, cultures, sexual orientation, and religious beliefs. Dr. Rushworth Kidder, the head of the Institute for Global Ethics, has researched the subject of shared worldwide values extensively. He says there are eight values upon which we all agree:

- Love
- Truthfulness
- Fairness
- Freedom
- Unity
- Tolerance
- Responsibility
- Respect for life

Who could possibly be against any of these?

In his best-selling book, *The Book of Virtues,* William Bennett, a former Secretary of Education, wrote that our country is in great need of moral education – "the training of heart and mind toward the good." He makes a strong case for teaching our young people the following virtues:

- Self-discipline
- Compassion
- Responsibility
- Friendship
- Work
- Courage
- Perseverance
- Honesty
- Loyalty
- Faith

Would anyone in any country stand up and protest against their children being taught any of those virtues? Character Counts!, the organization founded by Michael Josephson, is based on the Six Pillars of Character. They are:

- Trustworthiness
- Respect
- Responsibility
- Fairness
- Caring
- Citizenship

Notice the overlap of values/virtues/character traits in the above three lists. The reason is simple. Whenever you ask a group of people anywhere in the world to come up with a list of traits they want their children to learn and to practice, they usually come up with some combination of traits mentioned in the three lists above. There *are* universal values on which we can all agree.

Obstacle #2 – "My plate is too full; no time for any new add-ons."

This is also a common and legitimate concern, especially if teachers don't understand what character education is. They get new responsibilities dumped on them regularly by the federal government, local governments, their school district, and their own school administration. Rightfully so, they often feel overwhelmed. Someone brings up character education, and they respond with, "Oh, no, not another new program!"

Response – Character education *is* the plate. It's neither new nor an add-on.

As explained earlier, character development is as old as education itself. The leaders in the field aren't trying to bring in something new; they're trying to restore one of the original two goals of education. The original "plate" had two parts: academics and character. Somewhere in the 1960s, half of that plate broke off. And we've been paying the price, both in our schools and in our society, ever since.

If you ask teachers who've been around for a long time about the biggest change they've seen in kids, they'll tell you that they see more self-centeredness, hear more filthy language, and experience more rude and disrespectful behavior. They also comment on having more students than ever without proper guidance or direction, and without a work ethic to sustain them in school or in life. Most alarming of all, they see a vast increase in mean-spirited and cruel treatment of classmates – as well as an escalation of self-destructive behaviors.

We're seeing the results of poor parenting, a consistent barrage of harmful messages from the media, and lack of character education in our schools. The good news is that many schools have turned this around by implementing well-thought-out character education programs at the beginning of the school year. Character education won't eliminate all our behavior problems, but it *will* greatly reduce them. It also will create a much nicer environment for both teachers and students.

Obstacle #3 – "We're under intense pressure to raise test scores. There's no time to run a character education program."

High-stakes testing hit all of our schools about five years before I left the classroom. During those five years, I saw first-hand what it did to both administrators and teachers. The pressure to raise scores is enormous, and it takes its toll on all educators who are involved. Politicians like test scores because they're easy to measure. Low scores are bad, high scores are good. It doesn't matter whether the test is a valid measurement of success in academics, and it doesn't matter whether the test questions are good or bad. Just get those test scores up.

While I'm all for accountability in our schools, I have grave reservations about both the test and the way it's administered. I'm confident that over time educators and politicians can improve the entire process. But the reality is that high-stakes testing is here to stay. With scores made public in the newspapers and administrators' jobs on the line, I can understand why many people in schools believe they have time for nothing else.

Response – Test scores and all other measurements of academic success will improve in schools that have a solid character education program in place.

There is now sufficient evidence, borne out by research, that academic performance is enhanced when the culture within a school is one of mutual respect, responsibility, cleanliness, and hard work. When the message is, "We take education seriously, we honor the rules, and we help each other succeed," an entirely new environment is created. It's an environment in which teachers enjoy teaching and students enjoy learning. One of the results is improved academic performance.

School officials who claim they don't have time for character education are missing two important points. The first is that making character development an integral part of the school ethos is not so time-consuming that it will place an extra burden on teachers. In fact, if it is done well, it will *lighten* their burdens. Most of the work of integrating character education into the curriculum is done within the first two weeks of the school year. That's when the tone is set, expectations are established, and procedures are put into place. The other point that's being missed is that schools simply can't afford to miss this wonderful opportunity to improve the campus climate, help their students develop more fully as persons, and make progress in academic performance.

Obstacle #4 – "Our principal has no interest in character education."

This is a valid concern because there are principals all over the country, who, for a variety of reasons, will not commit to character education. Early in the movement to bring it back to the schools, we learned that without strong leadership and commitment at the top of the school, the chances of a successful school-wide program are reduced significantly.

Response – There are two ways in which character education can be implemented without the leadership of the principal.

The first is "by committee." I know hundreds of teachers around the country who have done this. A small group of them attend a character education conference, obtain valuable ideas about how to implement a program, and get excited enough to commit to follow through. They go back to their school, explain to the principal that it's a win-win situation for everyone, and volunteer to be the leaders of the movement. This type of teacher-led character education has proven successful in many schools at all grade levels. It's not uncommon for the principal to come on board after seeing the climate of the school dramatically improve.

> *Never doubt that a small group of thoughtful committed citizens can change the world. Indeed, it is the only thing that ever has.*
>
> *– Margaret Mead*

The second way to implement character education without the principal is by using what I call the "island technique." Ironically, I taught at a school in which the principal had zero interest in character education. She said, "That's not our job," and my explanations as to why it *is* our job fell on deaf ears. To make matters more difficult, there was no one on our faculty who had any knowledge of character education in the early stages of its comeback. So I made my classroom an "island" of character education. I did everything I could to create an environment in which my students would flourish both personally and academically. They liked it, their parents liked it, and I liked it for one simple reason – it worked!

A principal in Georgia who attended one of my workshops several years ago made this telling remark afterwards: "What you do is so simple. If every teacher in your school did the same things, you'd have a school-wide program." What I did *was* simple. It's what the rest of this book is about.

Character education vs. fluff

A few pages back I made the statement that academic achievement will improve in schools that have a solid character education program in place. There's an important word in that statement: *solid*. Unfortunately, there are a lot of things being done in the name of character education that I would call "fluff." Many administrators and teachers have good intentions, but they treat character education as if it's all "fun and games" and a series "feel-good" activities. Putting up a few signs, having a Word of the Week, and reciting a daily character education message over the intercom do not constitute a solid program. I'm not opposed to any of these activities, but they need to be done within the context of a well-thought-out and planned program that has substance to it.

It's important to understand that there's no *one* way to establish a strong program. Many schools have bought into organized plans such as the one Character Counts! employs, and have been very successful with them. Other schools bring in leaders in the field to work with their staffs, then implement a program designed to meet their specific needs. Still other character education strategies have been implemented through the joint efforts of teachers, parents, and community members. The most essential thing is that the people involved do their homework first. There are now countless books, conferences, speakers, articles, and websites available.

Character education, to be sure, can be done ineffectively, as little more than slogans, banners, and adults urging kids to be good. But schools that do character education well – in a way that transforms school culture, the daily experience of students and staff – create an environment in which diligent effort, mutual respect, and service to others are the rule rather than the exception.

– Dr. Thomas Lickona
Character Matters

What research tells us about good schools and character education

A growing body of research supports the notion that high-quality character education can promote academic achievement.

– Jacques S. Benninga, Marvin Berkowitz
Phyllis Kuehn and Karen Smith

In February 2006, an article was published in the *Phi Delta Kappan* entitled "Character and Academics: What Good Schools Do." It was researched and written by the four people cited in the above quotation from the article. They concluded that good schools consistently do four things:

1 – "Good schools ensure a clean and secure physical environment."

Both the staff and the students take pride in maintaining their buildings and their grounds. This provides a clean and safe learning environment and creates a sense of security. Students feel better and behave better in a clean school.

2 – "Good schools promote and model fairness, equity, caring, and respect."

In this finding the emphasis is placed on the role of faculty and staff members. In the best schools, the adults who work in them practice what they preach. They consistently model and promote the virtues and attitudes they want to see in their students. They show a deep concern for the well-being and growth of them.

3 – "In good schools, students contribute in meaningful ways."

Students are far more likely to buy into anything good if they have some ownership in it. The authors found that the best schools provided their students with several opportunities to contribute to the positive environment. Some of the activities mentioned are "cross-age tutoring, recycling, fund-raising for charities, community clean-up programs, food drives, visitations to local senior centers, and so on." These opportunities not only give students ownership and a sense of responsibility, they give them a sense of purpose.

4 – "Good schools promote a caring community and positive social relationships."

The best schools form partnerships with as many groups from their community as they can. This includes parents, businesses, service organizations, senior citizens, and local government officials. They encourage people of all backgrounds to work together in helping kids succeed academically while becoming good citizens.

> *Children develop character by what they see, what they hear, and what they are repeatedly led to do.*
>
> *– James Stenson*

Good teachers form partnerships with parents

It takes parents, teachers, and students working together as a team to ensure a child's success.

– Barbara E. Kerr
President, California Teachers Association

Parents are teachers too

Classroom teachers often forget that most of their students have had live-in teachers since the day they were born. They're called parents. Sometimes these live-in teachers are the best and most important in a child's life. And, unfortunately, they can sometimes be the worst. Whether they're at one of these ends of the spectrum or somewhere in between, they play an important role in education.

I was completely oblivious to all of this when I began my teaching career. As a result, I missed some golden opportunities in my early years to learn more about my students, to get help, to be supported, to be encouraged, and to receive expressions of appreciation. When I did my teacher training, very little was ever said about the role of parents. It was a real oversight. So I started my career with this attitude: Parents need to do what they need to do at home, and I need to do what I need to do at school; our jobs are completely separate. I was naïve, ignorant, and dead wrong.

It finally dawned on me – after seeing parents do important volunteer work at the school, getting phone calls and notes of appreciation from them, and receiving requests for help with their kids – that we were all in this together. The longer I taught, the more I did to include the parents. And the more I did this, the more cooperation I received. I'm not claiming that all parents (especially in the public schools) are wonderful and supportive. But I *am* saying that when teachers let parents know that they're valued, and invite them to become partners in educating their kids, most of those parents respond favorably.

Four types of parents

From my perspective there were four types of parents. Keep in mind that I taught in a multi-ethnic public high school in the San Francisco area. A teacher in an exclusive private elementary school in New England might have a completely different perspective of parent types. But whether you teach in grade school or high school, public or private school, I think you'll be able to relate to the types described below.

1 – Ghost parents

These are the parents you never or rarely meet or have contact with. They don't call, they don't respond to teacher requests, and they don't ask questions. On the positive side, they don't meddle, complain, or cause problems. But on the negative side, they come across as if they don't care about their kid's education or about what's going on at the school. That might not be true, as they could have all kinds of legitimate reasons (language, illiteracy, other hardships) for not being involved.

There are very few of these types of parents in the private schools, but many in the public schools, especially if there are language barriers. At least 40 percent of my students' parents fell into this category in my last 15 years in the classroom. But I never stopped extending an invitation to them. I also spoke privately with the students of ghost parents to find out what was going on at home. It's possible to do this without embarrassing them, and it almost always results in a valid explanation. It also gave me a better understanding of some of my students.

2 – Helicopter parents

These are the parents who are constantly hovering over their child, the school, the administration, and especially the classrooms. Every teacher has some of them, no matter what the grade level is or whether the school is public or private. The good news is that they're involved. Maybe a little *too* involved at times, maybe a little bothersome at times. They often put too much pressure on their child to excel at all levels, and they often question and criticize decisions made by administrators and teachers.

But the most important thing to remember about helicopter parents is that they care. They may have personalities that we describe as compulsive (there are far worse flaws), but they can become supportive allies if handled properly. In my early years I saw them as annoyances, as meddlers, and I wasn't nearly as cooperative with them as I could have been. As I matured, I worked hard to develop a win-win relationship with them. Their concerns were genuine (even if sometimes unfounded), and I always let them know their interest was appreciated. It worked a high percentage of the time.

3 – Nightmare parents

Some of my colleagues called these people "parents from hell." Whatever name you want to ascribe to them, they can be a handful. You can't avoid them simply because they come with the territory. No teacher has escaped at least a few encounters with this type of parent. They come in a variety of forms. Some are out-of-control helicopter parents, some defend their kids no matter what they do wrong, some blame the teachers even when they do everything right, some are impossible to please, some are unbelievably negative and angry (a lethal combination), some sit by and do nothing as they're informed their kid is failing and then explode on the teacher when it finally happens, and some love to threaten lawsuits.

The good news is that the percentage of nightmare parents is extremely small. In my case it was less than one percent. But they do exist, and all educators have to learn to deal with them in the best way they can. Here are a few things I learned to do when dealing with this type of parents:

- Check with the other teachers who also have to deal with them. It's often reassuring to know that you're not the only one having problems. You also might gain some new insights on both the parents and the student.

- Document your encounters. As soon as you realize there's trouble, start keeping a written record of every occurrence between you and the parent. You might never need the record, but it's always safer to have one.

- Inform an administrator right away. At some point you might need the support of someone in authority at the school. It's always wise to give that person a "heads up" in the early stages of the problem, especially if you sense that you're dealing with an unreasonable person.

4 – Dream parents

One of the truths about human nature that we often forget is that the good people in the world far outnumber the bad people. It's just that the ones who cause problems get much more publicity. It's the same with parents. The nightmare parents can wreak havoc, drain us, and demand a lot of our attention. But never forget that they're greatly outnumbered by good and kind parents who'll always support you if you're doing your best in teaching their children.

By a conservative estimate, I would say that close to 60 percent of my parents were absolutely wonderful. As mentioned before, I didn't understand this in my early days of teaching simply because I wasn't paying attention. I was too overwhelmed with the awesome responsibilities of my job to realize that there were powerful partners out there just waiting for my invitation to help out. When I extended that invitation, the answer was always yes from these types of parents. It resulted in some powerful partnerships and some great friendships.

No one comes to the party unless they're invited

Teachers often complain that parents don't get involved in the education of their children. Research shows that most parents do get involved when they're treated as partners. It all begins with an invitation.

– Professor David Gleason

I've thought for many years that the word *invitation* is among the most positive in the English language. Invitations always make people feel good. Everyone loves being invited to events, even if they don't want to attend. Because the invitation says, "You're important, you count, you're wanted." Previously in this chapter, I used the words *invite* and *invitation* in reference to forming partnerships with parents. As education professor Gleason says in the quotation above, that's how the process begins.

My initial invitation to parents was in the form of a letter. It was sent home with the students, along with some other materials, as the first homework assignment of the year. The assignment was to give the letter, an explanation of my policies, a course description, and a page about respect and manners to their parents. On a separate sheet both parents (if there were two) were asked to provide me with contact information. There was also a section on the page in which they could ask and answer questions, express concerns, and let me know the best ways and times to reach them.

On the next few pages you'll find a copy of the letter and some of the other materials I sent home at the beginning of the 2000-2001 school year, my last in the classroom. It was written on a school letterhead. I did my best to make it personal, at least at the beginning and at the end, even though I usually had more than 150 students. Instead of typing, "Dear Parents and Guardians," I hand-printed their names. At the end of the letter, instead of signing my name on the original and copying it, I signed each letter in a blue felt tip pen. Yes, it was time-consuming, but it was worth the extra effort in making it more personal.

Woodside High School

September 5, 2000

Dear Mr. and Ms. Applegate,

The purpose of this letter is to introduce myself as one of **Sarah's** teachers. I also want to extend an invitation, share my philosophy of education, provide you with a brief course description, explain my policies, ask you a few questions, allow you to ask a few of your own, and establish open lines of communication.

Introduction – This is my 35th year teaching in the Sequoia HS District. I can assure you that I've lost absolutely none of my enthusiasm for the job. In fact, it seems to get better and better. I earned a Bachelor's and Master's degree in History at the University of San Francisco. I also earned a California Teaching Credential and a Doctorate in Education there, and did post-doctoral study at Stanford University. I teach Psychology, U. S. History, and American Government.

Invitation – The most important purpose in writing this letter is to invite you to join me as partners in teaching your son or daughter. Research shows that when parents and teachers work together, the result is a better education. I look forward to meeting you and working with you. Please remember to put October 12 on your calendar. It's Back-to-School Night. I'll be sending more information about it in the weeks ahead.

Philosophy of education – I believe strongly that schools and teachers exist for two equally important reasons. The first is help our students increase in knowledge – to give them the tools and skills they'll need to function well in a changing world. The second is to help them develop good character and become good citizens. As Martin Luther King, Jr. wrote, "Intelligence plus character – that is the true goal of education." In addition to upholding high academic standards, I'll be doing all I can to help my students develop good attitudes, be respectful, work hard, and be honest. In my opinion, these are the four main ingredients of good character.

Here's hoping for a good year. Please feel free to contact me at any time.

Sincerely,

Hal Urban

American Government
Course description

Government is a one-semester course. All 12th-grade students are required to both take and pass the course as a graduation requirement. Following are the units of study:

The origins of U.S. Government – Types of government throughout the world, colonial governments in our early history, attempts to unify the colonies, the American Revolution, Declaration of Independence, writing of the U.S. Constitution and Bill of Rights.

The political spectrum – Explaining the following terms: liberal, conservative, right, left, radical, reactionary, moderate, extremist, libertarian. How political parties originated in the U.S. What is the difference between a Democrat and a Republican? What other parties are there in this country?

The federal government – Executive branch: President, Vice-President, Cabinet departments, advisers; Legislative branch (Congress): House of Representatives, U.S. Senate; Judicial branch: U.S. Supreme Court, courts of appeal, U.S. district courts.

California state government – Executive branch: the governor and other state-wide executive officials; Legislative branch: Assembly and Senate; Judicial branch: California Supreme Court, state courts of appeal, Superior Courts in each county.

Local government – County government: Board of Supervisors and other elected officials; City government: City Councils, mayors, and other elected officials; Special districts: school districts, harbor districts, hospital districts, etc.

Law and the courts – The difference between federal and state law, the difference between criminal and civil law. How federal crimes are prosecuted by U.S. Attorneys, how state crimes are prosecuted by County District Attorneys. How people accused of crimes are defended. How the jury system works.

Government in the news – Current events will be an on-going unit throughout the semester. Students will be asked to identify levels (federal, state, local) of government and branches (executive, legislative, judicial) of government.

Guest speakers – Experts in the above areas will be invited on a regular basis. They will include political party workers, criminal and defense attorneys, judges, law enforcement officers, FBI agents, the mayor, our Assemblyman, a member of the County Board of Supervisors, and others.

United States History
Course description

United States History is a two-semester course. All 11th-grade students are required to take and pass both semesters as a graduation requirement. Following are the units of study for the fall semester:

Geography – Most American high school students are geographically illiterate. They don't know the difference between a city and a state and a region. Most of them have no clue what or where Chicago and Philadelphia are. They can't identify most of the states on a map, and they know little about significant landmarks. They will know these things at the end of the unit.

Current U.S. – The purpose of studying history is to help us understand the present. But most American high school students know little about their country beyond its pop culture. In this unit they'll learn about population distribution, our economic system, our system of government, leaders in government and business, our different faiths, and our different political beliefs.

Exploration and colonization (1492-1763) – Changes in Europe, worldwide exploration, colonization in the south (Jamestown), in the middle region (Pennsylvania) and in the northeast (New England), early attempts at self-rule.

Revolution and independence (1764-1788) – Problems with the mother country, the Declaration of Independence, the American Revolution, and the aftermath, including the writing of a new Constitution.

A new nation (1789-1825) – The administration of our first five presidents: Washington, Adams, Jefferson, Madison, and Monroe; the development of political parties, the writing of the Bill of Rights, the Louisiana Purchase.

Westward expansion (1826-1849) – The filling in from ocean to ocean, the land rush, the gold rush, the war with Mexico, take-over of the Oregon, Utah, and California territories.

Civil War and reconstruction (1850-1877) – The different cultures of the North and South, slavery, compromise, then war; the legacy of Abraham Lincoln, the bitter battle to reunite the country.

The industrial period (1865-1900) – The great industrialists (Rockefeller, Carnegie, J.P. Morgan, etc.) take over; the railroads, immigration, inventions, mass production, corporations, big banks, the rise of labor unions.

Theme: "People make history," is something one of my history professors told me. The emphasis will be on biographies of the people who shaped the country. Second semester will cover from 1900-2000.

Psychology
Course description

Psychology is a one-semester elective course open to seniors only. Students are not required to take it, and if they do, they're not required to pass it as a graduation requirement. Since there are many types of psychology, and we have only one semester, the focus will be on the psychology of personal growth and development. Following are the units of study:

Introduction to psychology – This is a brief unit defining psychology and the related social sciences such as sociology and cultural anthropology. It also covers some of the pioneers in the field – Sigmund Freud, Carl Jung, Ivan Pavlov – and the basic type of psychology – Freudian, behaviorism, humanistic, developmental.

Emotional intelligence – What does it really mean to be smart? That's a question Daniel Goleman asks in his groundbreaking 1995 book, *Emotional Intelligence.* He concludes that it's the ability to develop self-control and to develop good character. I'll be covering the highlights of his work.

Attitude is a choice – Viktor Frankl, a psychiatrist and Holocaust survivor, said that the last freedom we'll ever have is the ability to choose our own attitudes, no matter what the circumstances. Positive or negative, attitude is always a choice.

Communication and relationships – It's been proven many times that people with good communication skills do better in life. This unit covers the power of words, non-verbal communication, listening, and empathy.

The 7 habits of highly effective people – Stephen Covey's book of the same title has sold more than 10 million copies. These habits are worth knowing. Among them are being proactive, understanding others, living by personal principles, co-operating with others, thinking win-win, planning, and renewing ourselves.

Goal-setting for life – This unit begins with an assignment to write 10 lifetime goals. It ends with an assignment to write 100 lifetime goals. Hundreds of students have told me it's the most valuable thing they've ever learned in school. And it's the most enjoyable topic I've ever taught. Many of my students work on their goals and write new ones long after they leave Woodside High School. People with written, specific goals achieve far more than those without goals.

Theme of course – I have a large sign in my classroom that has only two words on it: **"CELEBRATE TODAY!"** I point to it every day and ask my students what we're celebrating. I urge them to use what they learn in psychology to find good in the world, in others, and in themselves.

CONTACT INFORMATION

This information is for my records only and will be kept confidential. Please answer only the questions you deem appropriate. If you have any questions for me, please write them on the back of this sheet. I will get back to you soon.

Name of student _____

Subject _____ Period _____

Name(s) of parents/guardians

_____

_____

Mailing address _____

City and zip code _____

Home phone number _____

Work phone numbers _____

Please indicate which number you prefer and the best times to call

_____

E-mail addresses _____

_____

PERSONAL INFORMATION

How would you rate your son/daughter in the following categories?

1 – Motivation:	High	Average	Low
2 – Manners:	High	Average	Low

Is there anything else you would like me to know about your son/daughter? If yes, please explain:

_____

_____

_____

A few explanations

You may have a few questions about the preceding page, as have others in my workshops. Here are the most common questions and the answers:

Why do you ask for contact information when the school has it on record?

Two reasons: One, I found school records to often be out of date and unreliable. Two, it saved me a lot of time and frustration to have up-to-date records readily available in my classroom.

Why do you ask about the student's motivation and manners?

During the many years I spent in the classroom, these seem to have been the two biggest concerns expressed by parents early in the year. "How do I motivate my son?" and "Please let me know about my daughter's manners. We've tried to bring her up the right way." Since I received these concerns from only some of the parents, I decided to find out how the others felt. The questions about motivation and manners led to some valuable family discussion. The responses also gave me insight into both the student and his/her family. It also was revealing when parents chose to ignore these questions.

How do parents rate their kids on motivation and manners?

Motivation: High – about 40%, Average – about 40%, Low – about 20% I found the parents' assessment to be pretty close to the truth. Many of those who marked their kids low in motivation also asked for help in motivating them.

What percentage of the parents shared additional information about their kids with you? What types of things?

More than one third of them wanted me to know something additional about their son or daughter. In about half of these cases, it was either about a learning difficulty, a health problem, or some emotional distress that had occurred recently. The other half had something good to say about their kids, particularly in respect to manners, work ethic, and goals for college.

My contact information

Along with the materials I sent home at the beginning of the year I enclosed a small slip of paper with my contact information on it. It looked like this:

Contacting Mr. Urban

Please feel free to contact me in one of the following ways. I'll always respond either the same day or the following day.

Mail: Woodside High School, 199 Churchill Avenue, Woodside, CA 94062

Phone: (650) 367-9750, ext. 6783

E-mail: h.urban@sequoia.org

Final two pages

One of the other pages I sent home covered my policies in detail. Because I feel this is one of the most important steps a teacher takes at the beginning of the year, I've devoted an entire chapter to it. See Chapter 13.

The final page covered manners and The Golden Rule. It was the result of some agreements my students and I reached about what was and what wasn't acceptable behavior in the classroom. A separate chapter is devoted to this issue also. See Chapter 5.

Reminder

I want to close this chapter by using one of teaching's most powerful tools: reinforcement. With all the energy and imagination you have, extend a warm and sincere invitation to your parents to become your partners.

> *When teachers and parents work toward forming a partnership, communicating regularly and respectfully, only positive things result.*
>
> *– Professor Donald Campbell*

Good teachers start teaching at the door

If you can reach 'em, you can teach 'em.

– Educational proverb

The most important thing I did as a teacher

I taught class about 900 times every school year – five per day for 180 days. Before each one of those classes started, I stood in the hallway near the door and individually greeted and welcomed each student into my classroom the same way I would greet and welcome a friend coming into my home. It was the most important thing I ever did as a teacher. It was also the simplest, least time-consuming, most enjoyable, and most energizing thing I ever did as a teacher.

Let me give you a little background on how it all began. My first year of teaching was absolutely overwhelming. I was starting my career with only one semester – one class, basically – of student-teaching experience; I was teaching three different subjects, two of which I hadn't taught before; I had 175 students in five classes; and in addition to trying to learn their names, I was trying to learn an entirely new system and the names of my colleagues. I frequently felt as if I was drowning in lesson planning, correcting tests and papers, keeping grade records, attending meetings, and returning phone calls. It seemed like a job for at least five people. I kept telling myself that if I put in the long hours of hard work necessary, it would all pay off. I was confident that no year would be as difficult as the first one. I was right. Teaching was always hard work, but never as hard as that first year.

I learned hundreds of valuable lessons about teaching during that first year. The most important one came with about two days left. My U.S. History students were turning in their textbooks to me, one at a time, at my desk in the back of the room. I was to look over the book, OK its condition, and put it on a cart for the library. April Madden was the third person to turn in her book. As I was glancing at it, I looked up at her and had a troubling thought. Here was a girl who had attended my class about 180 times, and I knew almost nothing about her. I knew where she sat, I knew she got a C each semester, and I knew that she never once asked a question, answered a question, or took part in a discussion.

After spending so much time with her in the same room day after day, it was a disturbing realization. What was even more disturbing was the realization that there were probably more than a hundred other students in the same situation as April – I hardly knew them. I managed to forgive myself because the year had been so challenging and demanding, but I also vowed that I would figure out a way to make a better connection with my students and to personalize my teaching more the following year. During that summer, in addition to recovering from the trauma of my first year in the classroom, I did as much reading as I could about various approaches to teaching. Of all the things I read, this is what stuck with me the most:

> *Never let the demands of your job or the curriculum cause you to forget that each one of your students is a feeling–thinking human being. For education to be effective, it must be personal.*
>
> *– George Isaac Brown*
> **Human Teaching For Human Learning**

The question was: How do I make education more personal without losing a lot of academic time? This haunted me throughout the summer. Then, on Labor Day weekend, just before school started for my second year, a light went on as the result of entertaining some friends. My wife and I had invited a couple we were good friends with to our home for dinner. When the doorbell rang, I got up and went to the door to greet them. I hugged Elaine, shook hands with Robert, and welcomed them in as warmly as I could. That's when the light went on. I guess I had been thinking about the new school year and asking myself how I was going to make a better connection with my students. Now I had the answer. I would stand near the door, greet each student individually, and welcome him or her into my class as warmly as possible. Not only would I do it on the first day of school, but every day of the year, in every class.

Meeting a basic human need

Most experienced educators are probably familiar with Abraham Maslow's Hierarchy of Needs theory. This famous psychologist tells us that all humans have basic needs. When they're met, we move on to a higher level of needs. He says our most basic needs are physical: air, water, food, sleep, and shelter. If these are met, our next need is safety – living in a secure and predictable environment. A high percentage of children growing up in this country have their physical and safety needs met. But sadly, too many of them never have their third level of needs met. Often referred to as our need for love, it includes belongingness, affection, acceptance, and friendship. Far too many of our students aren't receiving these at home, and to make matters worse, they aren't receiving them at school, either.

Teachers can do some simple things to help kids feel as though they belong, that they're accepted, and that they count. It all begins with literally reaching out to them at the beginning of each class or school day. A sincere and warm greeting says, "I'm glad you're here. You're important." Dale Carnegie, in his classic book, *How To Win Friends And Influence People*, says the key to dealing effectively with people and to bringing out their best is to make them feel that they count. To make his point he quotes one of the greatest and most influential educators of all time:

The deepest urge in human nature is the desire to be important.

– John Dewey

What to expect on the first day

I was excited about the first day of school in my second year for two reasons. First, I had that overwhelming first year behind me, and I was confident that this one would be quite a bit easier. Second, I was going to greet my students at the door, and I was confident that all of them would not only appreciate my reaching out to them, but that they would return the greeting with energy and warmth. How wrong I was. Keep in mind that I was both idealistic and naïve in those early days of my career. While I never lost any of my idealism, I *did* lose a lot of the naïvety simply by gaining experience. My initial greetings turned out to be a disappointing, but valuable, experience.

I greeted more than 170 kids on the first day of school, and less then 20 percent of them (about 30-35) responded the way I thought they would. This small number of students looked me in the eye, smiled brightly, and accepted my extended hand as I introduced myself and asked them for their names. This is what I thought all of them would do, but it wasn't the case. The other 80 percent of the students avoided eye contact (most of them looking at the floor), gave me a dead-fish/limp-wrist handshake, mumbled something unintelligible, and rarely smiled. I was as surprised as I was disappointed. How could they not appreciate a teacher who was going out of his way to be friendly and welcoming on the first day of school? That was my issue, but the kids had another take on it.

The truth is, they'd never been greeted at the door by a teacher before, so they were unprepared for it. And as they later explained, some were even intimidated by me on that first day. They weren't used to having a big body – I'm 6–foot–5, 210 pounds – at the doorway to their classroom. An additional reason for the awkwardness at the door was the lack of social graces on the part of the kids. No one had ever taught many of them to make eye contact, give a firm handshake, and smile when meeting another person. That was the case back in September of 1967, and that's the case today. In fact, it's worse today.

My first impulse was to stop them at the door and say, "Hey, don't you realize I'm trying to welcome you into my class? Don't you see that I'm trying to make your education more personal?" But I set that impulse aside because it would have done more harm than good. Imagine the bad start we would have gotten off to if their introduction to the class included a little lecture on their inferior social skills from a very large man. So I just greeted each of them in the friendliest way I could, all the while thinking about how I could address the problem in a win-win manner. Little did I know that this was going to be the first "teachable moment" of the new school year.

Once I got everybody in, I made sure they were in the right place. I had my name, room number, and subject on the chalkboard, and I asked them to check their programs to make sure they had the same thing. Then I said, "Let me start the new school year with a little question. How many of you noticed where I was when you came into the room a few minutes ago?" Of course, they all knew where I was, even if some of them had acted like they didn't. One of the kids answered, "You were out in the hall by the door." I responded with another question: "Why do you think I was by the door?" The answer to that one was always the same: "You were at the door because it's the first day of school and you wanted to welcome us back." I said, "Good answer. It *is* the first day of school and I *do* want to welcome you back, and I also want to welcome any students who are new to the school. But there's a little more to it than that."

I said, "Let me apologize to some of you. I think I caught you off guard this morning by being at the doorway. I didn't want to make you feel uncomfortable. In fact, I was trying to do the opposite – to let you know you're welcome, and to make you feel comfortable in my class. My intentions were good." I also explained that my greeting wasn't a one-day deal. It would come every day of the school year. I said, "From now on, you'll be prepared for my greeting."

I also wanted to touch on the issue of eye contact, shaking hands, and smiling when meeting someone new. But I wanted to do it in a way that wouldn't make them feel like I was being critical. I said, "Let's talk about some basic social skills. How many of you were taught by your parents what do when you meet someone new?" About seven of them raised their hands. When I asked them what they'd been taught, they responded with three things: eye contact, a firm handshake, and a smile. One of the other kids in the class responded, "Oh, I was taught those things, too, but I didn't think they applied at school. Teachers don't usually greet us at the door." That was part of the problem. Kids often fail to make the connection between school and real life. I told them in the most positive way possible that all human beings, whether in school or in any other situation, deserved to be greeted politely. I said, "I know none of you meant to be rude to me this morning. That's why I wanted to talk about it. Remember, I'll be at the door to greet you every time you come to my class, and I want to make you feel as welcome as I would want a friend to feel when entering my home."

I'm convinced that it turned out to be a valuable lesson for many of my students. They were prepared to see me at the door the next day, and almost all of them gave me a smile, made eye contact, and gave me a firm handshake. And almost all of them appreciated what I was trying to do. I say "almost all" because there will always be a small percentage of kids who wish you were somewhere else – like at the chalkboard with your back to them, or in the bathroom. But even if these few greeted me with less enthusiasm than I would have liked, I still reached out to them every day as warmly as I could, and I always believed that I was teaching – and daily reinforcing – a valuable social skill.

Transferring energy

Many of my friends outside of the teaching profession frequently asked me questions about what it was like to be with teenagers all day long. I usually responded with something short and to the point, as in, "I absolutely love it!" And I did ... most of the time. The follow-up question was always the same: "What do you like the most about teaching?" And the answer was always the same: "The energy of the kids." That's a given in our profession, whether you're teaching first-graders or 12th-graders. Almost all kids have an enormous amount of energy, and I always felt it was my job to help them channel that energy in positive ways.

Not all of my colleagues felt the same way. I often heard other teachers at my school say something like this, in a groaning tone of voice: "Oh, those kids! They have so much energy; they just drain me." These were often teachers who were much younger than I and had been teaching far fewer years. I had to resist the temptation to say, "I think you're in the wrong profession. That's what teaching is – dealing with kids and their high energy levels. Their high energy level is part of the job description."

The word *drain* means to pull down or out, as in water that goes down the drain. I always felt the opposite about kids and their energy. They never drained me. They *infused* me. I used to tell them that when I was standing at the door waiting for them to come down the hallway, I was like a rechargeable battery. If I received 30 to 35 positive greetings at the door before each class, I would be completely charged and energized. This was the literal truth. After being on the receiving end of so many smiles and warm greetings, how could I not be fired up as I began class? How could I not want to give those students the best I had? The benefits of this brief energy–transferring session at the door were immeasurable. After only a few days, I couldn't even imagine teaching a class without first welcoming my students and receiving their positive charges.

Other greeting options

While my five daily greeting sessions out in the hallway always seemed to have a magical effect, after about a month I began to wonder if my students thought a handshake every day was a little bit too formal. I'd been a teacher for more than a year and had a pretty good reading of the culture the kids had created. One of the things I noticed was that the ways in which they greeted each other were much different than the ways adults greeted one another.

There seemed to be two sets of greeting rituals – one for the boys and one for the girls. The one I got the biggest kick out of was what the girls did if they hadn't seen each other for at least 10 minutes: they screamed! They were genuinely excited to see one another, and their facial expressions showed it. I also noticed that the girls touched each other more often, hugged, occasionally walked arm-in-arm, and their body language was generally more animated. The boys had a different set of greeting rituals. They gave high fives and low fives. They bumped knuckles and elbows. They gave each other macho handshakes, sometimes accompanied by some sort of primal grunt. They slapped each other on the back, and they often just bumped each other with their shoulders. It seemed to be their way of saying, "You're my friend, I like you, and I have a need to express my affection physically, but only in a macho or cool way."

As I daily watched many of the students on campus greet one another in these informal but friendly ways, I decided to add some options to my greetings at the door. A couple of months into my second year of teaching, I told my students I wanted to try something a little different. The first response I got was, "You're still going to greet us each day, aren't you?" I assured them I was, but that I wanted to add a little variety. We had a discussion about the ways in which they greeted each other, and we covered all of them. I told them I'd be in the same place each day, and that we still had two minimum standards for greeting each other. The first was eye contact, the second was a smile (if possible).

The option came with the physical part of the greeting. I told them if they preferred to continue to shake hands it was fine. But if they wanted to greet me in a less formal way, that also was OK. The most important aspect of this change was that the type of greeting would be their choice, and I would respond in the same manner. I assured them I could high five, low five, bump knuckles, shoulders, or elbows, hug them, or respond to any other appropriate greeting. I also urged them to not do anything that made them feel uncomfortable.

I wasn't really sure what would happen the next day, but I was pleasantly surprised. The energy level seemed to be even higher than usual, and the kids genuinely enjoyed greeting me more in their style. I received a wide variety of greetings that day, including several hugs. That delighted me because it said that the kids liked and trusted me enough to greet me that way. The more we progressed into the school year, the more hugs I received. It was wonderful. I can't think of a warmer or more affectionate way of greeting another person. A non-teaching friend asked me one day what was so great about teaching. I said, "Well, there aren't too many jobs in which you can get hugged as many as a hundred times a day."

I found out later that for many of the kids, it was the only hug they received that day. I found this sad because I'd assumed that all families expressed their affection with one another. I was both naïve and wrong. The simple truth is that people of all ages need affection, and teachers need to express that affection whenever possible and appropriate. Kids needed affection back in the 1967-68 school year, which is when I started hugging them, and they need it even more today. Some of them are starving for genuine affection.

I frequently get asked during workshops with teachers if I ever got any complaints about hugging the kids. I'm pleased to say that in 34 years of doing it, I never received a single complaint. Not from a student, not from an administrator, not from a parent. In fact, when I greeted the parents in the hallway on Back-to-School Night, they frequently asked, "Do we get a hug, too?" I always said, "Yes, if you want one." And many did give me a hug, even though it was, in many cases, the first time we'd met. I loved it.

Hugging isn't for everyone

I can't emphasize enough how important it was to allow the kids to *choose* the method with which they greeted me. To hug them when they didn't want to be hugged would have led to nothing but problems – and probably the end of my career. There are a lot of important variables that must be considered when it comes to methods of greeting. Some of them are community standards, district and school policies, the ages of the students, and the sex, age, body shape, and personality of the teacher.

Let me provide you with a few examples:

1) I have a friend who teaches high school in North Carolina. His district has a strict policy about *not* hugging students. While he'd like to hug many of the kids, he honors the policy. But he also greets them at the doorway every day in a variety of friendly ways. He also teaches them about eye contact and smiles.

2) In a number of workshops, young and attractive female teachers have asked me if they should hug their students. My first question is always, "At what level do you teach?" When the answer is, "I teach in high school," I smile, shake my head, and say, "Absolutely not!" I can't help imagining some 16-year-old boy with raging hormones. If he had the invitation to hug his attractive young female teacher every day, he'd do it with gusto. In fact, he'd probably hold on a little too tightly and a little too long, then

brag about it to his friends. Too tempting, too risky. There are safer ways to greet kids under those circumstances.

3) What about a young male high school or junior high teacher? Should he hug the girls? While I wouldn't say, "Never!," I *would* say, "Be careful." The truth is, girls at this age do develop crushes on some of their young male teachers. The teacher needs to be aware of this, and he needs to be professional at all times. If in doubt, don't. I'm sorry if this different advice for young women and young men comes across as sexist, but the truth is, it's different. The raging hormones of a teenage boy are simply more fraught with potential problems.

4) I have a friend named Helen who teaches junior high school in the St. Louis area. You need to know what she looks like: she's in her 60s, has a full head of gray hair, is a plus-size woman, and is extremely buxom. I'm not being critical in any way. In fact, I asked her if it was OK to describe her in this way. Because she has a wonderful sense of humor, she laughed and said, "You're being more polite than you need to be. Just say I'm old and fat." Regardless of what terms I use, you need to have a picture of Helen to see what her junior high students see each day. Do you think they'd be comfortable getting a hug from her? By the way, they love her. She's an incredibly enthusiastic and popular teacher, and she's won many awards. She greets all her students at the door on the first day of school. Not surprisingly, many of them look at the floor when being greeted by her. This is what she says to them once everyone gets into the room: "I'll be at the door to greet you before every class. You *will* look me in the eye, you *will* smile, and you *will* say, 'Good morning, Ms. Nelson.' Because if you don't, I'll hug you."

She gets a polite greeting from all of her students every day.

The build-up effect

Earlier in this chapter I wrote about April Madden, a student I had in my first year of teaching. By the end of the year I hardly knew her, and I hardly knew a lot of my other students. Think how different it would have been for April and the others had they been in my U.S. History class one year later. I would have greeted them and introduced myself on the first day of school. And to follow up that initial meeting, I would have greeted them each succeeding day – about 180 more times.

Each time I greeted them, I would know a little more about them than the day before, and the connection between us would grow stronger. I would know more about them because I had my students fill out a personal information sheet during the first week of school. You'll find a copy of it in Chapter 6. It allowed me to know more about my students and their interests. It also allowed me to engage them in brief conversations that were personal to them. This is what I mean by the build-up effect. I knew them a little better each time they came to my class.

What about the roaming teacher?

One of the most frequently asked questions in my workshops comes from teachers who don't have the luxury of having a classroom to call their own. Some teachers, especially those without a lot of seniority, move from room to room. I was in the same position for my first five or six years of teaching. It meant that I would teach in one class, gather up my materials, and head for the next classroom, which could be all the way across the campus. If the students were already in the room by the time I got there, it was a little difficult to welcome them at the door.

There's a surprisingly simple solution to this problem, and it includes options for the students. I told them they were likely to get to the room before I did. They were welcome to go in and sit down if that's what they felt like doing. They were also given the option of hanging out near the door with their friends until I got there for the greeting. When I got to the room, I greeted those who were outside waiting for me. Then I went in and individually greeted each of the students who were already in the room. Problem solved. It wasn't as good as always being at the door before they came, but it worked, and they appreciated the effort I was making to reach out to them. Where's there a will, there's a way.

Saying good-bye

For junior high and high school teachers, establishing a greeting ritual on the first day of school is critically important. Because classes are usually short and because there's so much movement between classes, it isn't always possible to say good-bye in the way we'd like. But for elementary school teachers who are with their students either all or most of the day, I highly recommend an end-of-the-day good-bye ritual as well.

I have a friend who teaches third grade in a school near the high school at which I taught. She invited me to her classroom once so I could see how she ended each school day. She introduced me to the children, and I took a seat in the back of the room to watch her. About five minutes before the bell she said, "Children, it's time to say good-bye for the day." They all stood up and, in an orderly fashion (they rotated the order each day), formed a line. She sat in a chair near the doorway so she would be at eye level with them. Each child approached her one at a time, looked her in the eye, smiled, either shook hands or hugged her, and said some variation of this: "Good-bye, Mrs. Shields. Thank you for teaching us today. Have a nice evening." So simple, yet so powerful.

A final word about greeting students at the door

Because I'm a teacher, I like to repeat things, especially things that I think are important. In education, we call it *reinforcement.* Or as I learned during one of the first days in teacher training, *Repetitio est mater studiorum.* It's Latin for "repetition is the mother of learning." This is what I said in the first paragraph of the first page of this chapter about greeting my students: "It was the most important thing I ever did as a teacher. It was also the simplest, least time-consuming, most enjoyable, and most energizing thing I ever did as a teacher. "

When students feel welcome and connected, they feel more at home, more like they belong. This is critically important because everyone functions better in a comfortable environment.

– Professor Joseph Napier

Good teachers teach manners and the Golden Rule

*If manners were an animal, it would be an
endangered species.*

*– Henry C. Rogers
Public relations expert*

The second most important thing I did as a teacher

I opened the previous chapter by saying that greeting my students at the door before every class was the most important thing I did as a teacher. Teaching them about manners and the Golden Rule on the first day of school was a close second. This wouldn't have been true during my first 15 or so years of teaching. I hardly ever mentioned manners for one simple reason: it wasn't necessary. Kids came to school on time and regularly. They were dressed well (we had a dress code), they were generally respectful, said "please" and "thank you," and if they swore, they did it privately or in the parking lot. Oh my, how things have changed since the early days of my career!

The decline of manners and civility was the single biggest change I saw during my 35 years in the classroom. And I'm not referring only to school-age kids. I'm talking about people of all ages. The way kids talk and act will always be a reflection of what's going on in popular culture, and of what they see and hear from the adults around them. In many cases this means their parents. That can be good or bad.

When I do workshops with teachers around the country, an important part of every presentation has to do with how I dealt with our manners crisis. I always ask the veteran teachers if they've seen a decline in respect and courtesy in the years they've been teaching. One hundred percent of them say yes. I ask them if most kids of all ages do rude and inconsiderate things. Again, the answers are all yes. Then I ask another question that's a little more thought provoking. I share with them that I have two theories on kids and manners, and I want to see if they agree with me. The first is that kids are a reflection of what's going on around them in the adult world, with particular emphasis on the entertainment industry. My second theory is that about 90-95 percent of the time in which kids are being rude, they don't even know they're being rude. They're acting out of ignorance. Not stupidity, but ignorance – simply not knowing any better. Why? Because no one has taught, reinforced, or trained them in what used to be known as common courtesy. I ask teachers if they agree with my theories. Virtually all of them do. The more important question is: Can we do anything about it? The answer is YES!

"What you accept, you teach"
"What you permit, you promote"

I learned something invaluable about classroom management during my second year of teaching. I was required to attend an after-school workshop conducted by a former teacher who had become a legend in our school district. He started teaching in the 1930s and retired in June of 1966, three months before I arrived on the scene. He had won just about every award they can give to a teacher. He was what we call a "Tough Love" teacher. He was strict without being mean, wasn't afraid to make students work, had a wonderful sense of humor, and had a special way of letting his students know that he cared about them. He had a rich combination of the most important qualities of a successful teacher.

These are the words with which he opened the workshop: "What you accept, you teach." I had no idea what he meant, and neither did anyone else in the room. He said, "Now that I've started off by confusing you, let me explain that this was the most valuable bit of advice I received back in the 1930s when starting my own teaching career. One of the veteran teachers on my own staff said this to me the day before classes started. I didn't know what it meant, either, but I learned in a hurry." He went on to explain that if a student does something unacceptable in your classroom, whether it's rude, mean-spirited, or simply against the rules, you must deal with it immediately. If you ignore it, you're essentially accepting it as permissible. You're also teaching that student, and all of his or her classmates, that it's OK to behave this way in your class.

He said you *must* deal with these infractions as soon as they occur. The most important thing is the manner in which you do it. He advised us to not lose our composure, to not yell at the student, and to not make him or her look bad in the presence of classmates. He said, "You can be firm and loving at the same time. Students need to know early on that you're in charge, they need to know what your standards and expectations are, and they need to know what will not be tolerated." He added, "Everyone operates more effectively when their boundaries are clearly defined." It was one of the best workshops I ever attended.

In 2004, I learned a new, and possibly better, version of "What you accept, you teach." I made a presentation to the faculty at Mt. Olive High School in New Jersey. Teaching manners, as always, was an important part of it, so I shared what I'd learned at that workshop way back in 1968. Afterwards, Kevin Stansberry, the dynamic young principal, said he'd never heard "What you accept, you teach," but he used a phrase that meant the same thing. His version is "What you permit, you promote." I thought it was outstanding, and I've been sharing it with teachers ever since. It doesn't make any difference which one you use or if you use both, but I do suggest that you plant this concept firmly in your mind. Remind yourself often that you set the tone, that you're in charge. Let your students know in a firm and loving way that you have high expectations, and that you'll hold them to high standards.

People behave as they're expected to behave.

– Sociology 101

Be proactive, not reactive

Act or be acted upon.

– Stephen R. Covey

I took a sabbatical leave during the 1990-91 school year to write my first book, *20 Things I Want My Kids to Know* (since changed to *Life's Greatest Lessons: 20 Things That Matter*). After 15 months away from the classroom, I was anxious to get back to teaching. I found myself totally unprepared for the change in student attitudes and behavior. Not in all of the students, but in an alarmingly high number of them. At first I thought it was me. Maybe I'd gone a little soft while staying in the comfort and quiet of my home for a year, writing every morning and taking a little snooze almost every afternoon. I'd forgotten how loud schools are, and how much commotion goes on daily. But those are part of the territory known as teaching, so I made the necessary readjustment quickly.

I didn't adjust as well, however, to the decline in manners. And I found out that it wasn't just me. After talking to several of my colleagues, I discovered that we were of the same belief that "common courtesy" wasn't so common any more, particularly at school. All of the teachers were struggling with this change, and many, including me, longed for the "good old days." I found myself calling "time out" with much greater frequency than before. Each time was for the same reason – to correct some form of inconsiderate behavior that I rarely had to deal with in previous years. What bothered me the most was the frequency of these little rudeness eruptions. I felt like we were wasting a lot of class time. I also felt like putting a bumper sticker on my chalkboard that said, "I'd rather be teaching."

It finally dawned on me that I was treating the issue in a *reactive* manner. I was waiting until a student did something wrong, then *reacted* to it. It's always a challenge (and always uncomfortable) to correct a kid in front of his or her peers. But it has to be done if the behavior is unacceptable. It's important to do it gently and constructively, but a teacher still runs the risk of embarrassing and/or alienating the student. I started thinking that this was happening too frequently, that it was wasting too much valuable class time, and that there must be a more effective way of dealing with the problem.

It was about that time that the word "proactive" was being used extensively in the business world. I kept coming across it in the textbooks and other materials I used to teach Organization Behavior courses to working adults at the University of San Francisco. Basically, it means taking a positive step up front to head off trouble instead of waiting for something negative to happen and then reacting to it. I decided to take a proactive approach to the manners issue. That meant dealing with the issue on the first day of school. Maybe I could teach some of my students the rewards of mutual respect and what used to be known as common courtesy. Maybe I could convince them that it would result in a more pleasant classroom atmosphere and a win-win situation for all of us.

So after greeting them at the door and having our discussion about the importance of having good social skills, I told them that my No. 1 goal for the year was to create, with their help, the best possible environment in my classroom. I told them I wanted it to be a place in which they always felt welcome, by both their classmates and me. I also wanted it to be a place in which they would always feel confident that both their classmates and I would treat them with respect. To be more specific, I wrote the following on the chalkboard:

Choosing an atmosphere	
Rude	Courteous
Inconsiderate	Considerate
Disrespectful	Respectful
Offensive	Polite

If you're familiar with any of my four other books, you'll know that I place great emphasis on one's power to choose. As teachers we need to be constantly showing and reminding our students that they have choices, and that those choices will determine the quality of their lives. I'll refer to the freedom and power of choice often in the remaining pages of this book. In this particular case, I wanted to show my students that the atmosphere we created together would determine the quality of life in my classroom, and that it was a matter of choice.

It may seem like a complete no-brainer, but after writing the above words on the board, I asked them to choose the atmosphere they wanted. I asked, "What'll it be? Left or right?" I don't think it will surprise you that they chose the words on the right. Doing it this way is far more effective than simply asking, "Do you want a bad atmosphere or a good atmosphere?" The purpose of putting specific words on the board and pointing out that we could choose our atmosphere helped my students conceptualize the issue much more clearly. It also helped them realize that they shared the responsibility with me for creating a positive environment in the classroom.

When I returned to teaching in 1991 after my sabbatical leave, I had 16 years of teaching experience. I asked my students to guess what the biggest change was that I'd seen in kids during that time. "It must be manners," said Sean, an insightful junior. I said, "You're right. I'd like to know what your views are on the subject." They had more to say that I thought they would.

It surprised me that so many of my students agreed that there'd been a serious decline in respectful behavior at school. They were of the strong opinion that there was way too much rudeness and disrespect going on regularly in most of their classes. What was most surprising, however, was that they criticized the teachers for rarely doing anything about it. They thanked me for bringing it up.

I'd actually been concerned about how the students would respond to me discussing the issue of manners on the first day of school. I envisioned hearing comments like, "Ah, c'mon, Mr. Urban, you're showing your age. Kids are different these days. It's a new generation," or, "We're not in kindergarten, you know." But instead I was actually being *thanked* for bringing up an issue that not only was important to me, but to them as well.

One of the students said, "Maybe if all the teachers discussed this on the first day of school, some of the manners would improve around this place." It was my opening. I said, "Let me give you a page that might help us get the year off to a good start." Here's what I gave them:

WHATEVER HAPPENED TO GOOD MANNERS?

Without good manners, human society becomes intolerable and impossible.

– George Bernard Shaw
Irish playwright, 1800s

How things were different not too many years ago:

1 – Students rarely came to class late. When they did, they apologized. Today many often come late. Only rarely does one apologize.

2 – Students didn't get up, walk across the room to throw something in the wastebasket, and walk back across the room while the teacher was talking to the class. Today it is done often.

3 – Students didn't litter the classroom or write on the desks. Today many students do both.

4 – Students didn't talk back to teachers in a defiant manner. Today it frequently occurs.

5 – Students didn't swear in the classroom or in the hallways. Today some students can't talk *without* swearing.

6 – Students would say, "May I please have …" in a pleasant tone of voice if they needed something from the teacher. Today many students say, "I need …" often in a demanding, demeaning, and disrespectful tone of voice.

7 – Students used to say "thank you" to teachers who helped them. Today only a few students bother to thank teachers.

8 – Students used to listen when the teacher was talking. Today many students feel they have the right to ignore the teacher and have a private conversation with their friends.

9 – Students listened when a classmate had something to say. Today many students don't bother to listen to their classmates.

10 – Students, in general, were more considerate of other people's feelings. Today many students could care less about other people's feelings. They're more "into themselves."

After handing out the page, I simply asked my students to look it over and then give me some feedback. Questions, concerns, ideas, suggestions – whatever came to mind. I'll always remember the first comment I ever heard when using this page. Tracy, a very polite and gracious senior, said, "It sure must have been easier and more pleasant to teach in the old days. Teachers have to put with so much rude behavior today. I can't believe some of the things students are allowed to get away with now." My response was that teachers *shouldn't* have to put up with rude behavior and that students *shouldn't* be allowed to get away with it. I said that I wanted to address the issue on the first day of school so we could do everything possible to create a good atmosphere. I concluded by saying, "Mutual respect is always win-win."

Another observation the students shared with me was what most teachers did on the first day of school. They made a seating chart, handed out a course description that included grading policies, and handed out a set of class rules. Most of the rules started with the words, "You are not allowed to ..." There was never a discussion about manners, courtesy, mutual respect, or the importance of creating a good atmosphere in the class. I had learned early in my career that making a seating chart, handing out course descriptions, policies, and rules on the first day of school was *not* the best way to begin a school year. Greeting the kids at the door and asking them to join you in creating an atmosphere of mutual respect is far more effective in getting the year off to a good start.

The most common example of bad manners in the classroom – and how to fix it

Earlier in this chapter I listed 10 things kids used to do politely and 10 things they're now doing rudely. Please take another look at No. 6. Kids rarely ask for things politely these days. Instead, they *demand* things. This is by far the most frequently repeated example of poor manners in the classroom. The saddest aspect of it is that so many teachers allow it to go on, day after day, without making any effort to correct it in a constructive way.

Consider the following scenario. It's the 1978-79 school year, and I'm in my 13th year of teaching. Much earlier in my career, I'd earned the affectionate nickname of "The Handout King." I probably had a few other nicknames, but we'll stick with this one for now. I'd discovered early on that I disliked textbooks as much (and maybe more) as the kids did, so I started developing my own materials for each course that I taught. I was easily able to convince my students that my handouts were more interesting than a textbook, that they got to the point quickly and directly, and that they were easier to understand. I told them they would need a three-ring binder, and to help them stay organized, I would punch holes in the left side of the paper and number each one in the upper right-hand corner. The bottom line: a handout was a good thing.

So let's say we're in the third week of the school year in my U.S. History class in September of 1978. We've completed all of our beginning-of-class rituals (to be discussed in Chapter 9), and we're ready to go to work. The first thing I do is a "binder check" to see if everyone has the last page that was handed out. So on that particular day I say, "Please check your binders. We're now up to page 14."

Adam had been absent the day before and was missing the last page. He politely raises his hand, I acknowledge him, and he says, in a respectful tone of voice, "Mr. Urban, I was absent yesterday and missed the last page. May I please have page 14?" I respond by saying, "You sure can," and hand him the page. He responds in turn by saying, again in a respectful tone, "Thank you, Mr. Urban." And I respond by saying, with a smile and a tone that shows my appreciation for his good manners, "You're welcome."

What did we call this little transaction? Common courtesy. But that isn't what's happening in most schools today. Now let's fast-forward 10 years to the 1988-89 school year and the same scenario – third week of school in a U.S. History class. I do my binder check and announce that we're up to page 14. Scott was absent yesterday. He doesn't raise his hand. He just blurts out, "I need page 14." He says it in a demanding and demeaning tone of voice. Some students even add a little word in front of "I need ..." The word is "Hey," making the demand even more disrespectful. The main difficulty with this is that so many of the kids are in the habit of saying, "I need ..." I can only conclude that they say it at home and get what they want instead of being corrected. Then they bring it to school – and still don't get corrected.

You'll recall that I previously explained that "What you accept, you teach," and "What you permit, you promote." This is a perfect example. If Scott says, "I need page 14," in a demanding tone, and I give it to him, then I've accepted his way of asking for (or demanding) things. I teach him and all of his classmates a simple lesson: "This is the way you ask for things in my class. You can be demanding and disrespectful, and I'll still get you what you want." So the rudeness and bad habits continue.

You solve the problem by addressing it on the first day of school, *before* it happens. I literally acted out both of the scenarios described above so the students could get a picture of both politeness and rudeness, so they could hear both the polite and rude tones of voice. I would say this to them: "Please don't demean me by asking for things in a demanding way. I know you may be in the habit of asking for things that way, and I know you don't mean to be rude, but the truth is, it *is* rude." I told them that if they demanded something of me I would look at them, smile, and then act like I didn't hear them. I might even cup my ear with my hand. That was a signal for them to rethink what they just said and how they said it, and to then try again. They got it. And they made a conscious effort to ask for things politely.

Three ways of communicating

This always seemed like the perfect time to help my students understand that we usually use three different methods of communication when talking to one another:

1 – Words – About 10-15 percent of our message

2 – Tone of voice – About 40 percent of our message

3 – Body language – About 45-50 percent of our message

This helps them understand just how dramatically different it is between saying, "I need ..." in a demanding tone with a scowl, and saying, "May I please have ..." in a pleasant tone with a smile.

Some discussion questions about manners and the Golden Rule

In addition to the list of things kids used to do and the things they're doing now, I had a few more items for discussion. I also gave my class these questions:

1) Why have manners and civility declined so much in the past 20 years?

2) Is society better when people treat each other with respect?

3) Is a classroom better when both students and teacher show mutual respect?

4) Why does Henry Rogers, a public relations expert, say, "Good manners are one of the most important keys to success in life"?

5) What is the Golden Rule? If it sounds so good and is so easy to understand, why don't more people practice it?

6) What are parents teaching kids about manners these days at home? Do those manners apply at school? Are there any places in which they *don't* apply?

My students were always more than willing to discuss these questions, but they didn't understand No. 5. Many of them had never heard of the Golden Rule. Ah, another teachable moment (the first one came from greeting them at the door) – and it's still the first day of school! In the old days, every student knew what the Golden Rule was. It was common knowledge. But it's gone the way of common courtesy. Very few students today know what the Golden Rule is. So I wrote the following on the board:

Treat others the way you'd like them to treat you

I pointed out that it *doesn't* say, "Treat people the way they're treating you." The Golden Rule calls upon us to take the high road – to be kind and respectful even when others aren't. I also asked them if they knew who said it and where it could be found. There were usually a few students who knew it was in the Bible and that Jesus said it (Matthew 7:12 and Luke 6:31). But they didn't know that many other people also had said it, many of them before Jesus. For example, Confucius said the following about a thousand years earlier: "Don't do to others what you don't want them to do to you." Literally hundreds of people have been saying essentially the same thing for thousands of years. They come from different periods in history, different continents, different races and cultures, and different belief systems. Basically, the Golden Rule is a universal principle of good human relations.

I pointed out a large (four feet by six feet) poster that I had in the back of my room. A friend who made signs and posters for a living had made it for me. At the top it said, "The Golden Rule Throughout The Ages." Below it were 15 different versions of it, with a citation for each. The specific words were a little different in each version, but the meaning was the same. If you want to do something similar, all you have to do is a "Google" search on the Golden Rule. You'll find more than 15 versions. In fact, you'll find 21 from various religions and philosophies, five from specific philosophers, and two more from moral/ethical systems simply by clicking on the following website:

www.religioustolerance.org/reciproc.htm

The most important point to be made about the Golden Rule is that, regardless of what people's religious beliefs are, putting it into practice always results in a win-win situation. Someone once said, "If everyone lived by the Golden Rule, we probably wouldn't need any other rules." There's a lot of truth in that statement. It's not hard to understand or agree with the principle behind the Golden Rule, but it's a little more challenging to consistently practice it. When I asked my classes what the key was to consistently putting it into practice, the best answer I received was, "To always be considerate of other people."

Does the Golden Rule apply to substitute teachers?

Before leaving this important concept I had to put it to the test, to challenge my students to apply it in *all* circumstances. All I had to do was ask the question above. Because the Golden Rule was still just an intellectual concept to them, most of them had the same answer: "No way!" Somehow it's become ingrained into the psyches of school children of all ages that they're required to terrorize substitute teachers. I repeated the question in a few different ways: "If this was six years from now and you were the substitute teacher, how would you like to be treated by the students? If your older brother or sister, or your mom or dad, subbed in this class, how would you want the students to treat them?" The first response was actually somewhat amusing. One of the kids said, "Oh, that's different. Now you're talking about us and family members." My response was (complete with a smile), "No, I'm talking about treating others the way we'd like to be treated." They all got the point.

To make sure substitute teachers were treated well in my classes, I suggested that we give them a new title. "How about 'Guest Teacher?' And how are we supposed to treat guests?" Then I added a little more to the circumstances. I asked them if they'd ever gone someplace where they hardly knew anyone. They all had. I asked them if, in those circumstances, anyone had gone out of his or her way to reach out and make them feel welcome. Most had. I suggested that when I was gone and they realized they had a Guest Teacher, some of them might want to approach the guest, introduce themselves (another thing kids are not too good at) and say, "Welcome to Mr. Urban's class. Is there anything I can help you with?" Substitute teachers are blown away when this happens – in a good way. Imagine the impact if four or five or more of the students do this before class starts. The kids not only enjoyed it, they thought it was funny because the substitutes were so surprised. Some of them even wondered if they were being set up. One of them told me the next day, "It was like an out-of-body experience. I was wondering what was going on, when the boom was going to be lowered. Then it finally dawned on me that it was all for real. And it was wonderful!"

I received some beautiful notes over the years from my Guest Teachers. Most of them said something similar to this one, which I received in 1999: "Mr. Urban, Thanks for the clear lesson plan, and thanks especially for whatever you did to set the tone of respect in your class. You have the most polite students in the school. This was an absolutely delightful experience. If you ever need a substitute – I mean Guest Teacher – again PLEASE ask for me!" Signed, Shirley Cohen. What did I do with the note? I read it out loud to my students. I told them I was proud of them and added, "This is what I mean by the Golden Rule always being win-win."

One final story about manners –
because it's simply too good to leave out

In the early 1990s, one of my teaching colleagues told me that I would have a new student in my third period U.S. History class, starting in the Spring semester, which was only a few days away. He was a German exchange student who needed to make several changes in his program at the end of the first semester. The other teacher assured me that he was a great student and a fabulous kid, and that I would really enjoy having him in class. His name was Henning Austmann. Henning was the proverbial Teacher's Dream. He was personable, polite, and incredibly enthusiastic about learning everything he could about the United States during his one year in the country.

I met him on the first day of the new semester and introduced him to the other students, who'd been in the class since school started in September. It was an outstanding group of kids, and Henning fit right in. On Thursday of that first week, Henning hung around at the end of class instead of going to lunch. I asked him, "Aren't you going to lunch? Aren't you hungry?" He said he was, but that he wanted to share something with me before he went to lunch. I asked him, in my usual professional and articulate manner, "What's up?" He said, "You know, Mr. Urban, I've been in your class for four days now, and there's something I just have to tell you." I had no idea what it was, but Henning was such an upbeat and enthusiastic kid, I figured it would be something positive. I was right.

He said, "You are a very lucky teacher." I wasn't sure where he was going with this, but I answered, "Yes, Henning, I *am* a lucky teacher. I'm lucky just to *be* a teacher. I'm lucky to have found my calling in life. Is that what you mean, or are you referring to something else?" He said he was referring only to my third-period class. I said, "What do you mean?" He said, "Let me put it this way, Mr. Urban: I take six different classes at this school, and the students in third period are *by far* the most polite students in any of my classes. Mr. Urban, you are *so* lucky to have such polite students in third period."

I said, "Henning, you're right, they *are* very polite, and I *am* lucky to have them. But I should tell you something else. I teach five classes every day, and the students in all five of them are polite." He looked at me incredulously and said, "Wow! You're even luckier than I thought you were." He then asked me how this had happened. How did I luck out and get so many polite students in one year. I laughed. Then I said, "Henning, your English is very good. Have you ever heard of the word 'proactive'?" He hadn't. So I said, "Good, I get to teach you a new word today."

I explained to him what I always did on the first day of school regarding manners and about the pages I handed out. Of course, he wanted to see them. So I got them out and let him take a look. After studying them for a few minutes he looked up at me with an excited look on his face and said, "Mr. Urban, I've got a great idea for you!" I was curious, so I said, "Go ahead." He said, "Mr. Urban, call a faculty meeting. Get all the teachers up there in that multi-use room and teach them how to teach manners to their students." Oh boy, I thought, that would go over *really* well; me calling a faculty meeting so I could tell other teachers what they should be doing. As sincere as Henning was, I had to explain that it would never fly. I even quoted the Bible: "The teacher (prophet) is without honor in his own land." And then I gave him the definition of an expert: "someone who goes *out of town* to speak."

I would have loved to share with my colleagues how much better my classes were as a result of dealing with the manners issue on the first day of school. But the sad truth is that most teachers don't want to be told how to do things by another teacher on their own faculty. Fortunately, I *did* have the opportunity to share my strategies regarding manners and other areas of teaching with some of my fellow faculty members. I was a Mentor Teacher several times during the latter part of my career and was able to share many of the things I'd learned with first-year teachers. All of them agreed that the proactive approach to manners made a big difference in their classrooms.

Summary

You might be wondering how much time I spent on manners on the first day of school. It sometimes took 30 minutes. It sometimes took up most of the period. And it sometimes spilled over into the second day of school. It never mattered to me how long it took because I always knew the kids were getting something valuable out of it, and I knew my classes would be better because of it. I never saw it as losing time. I saw it as an investment in *gaining* time. I rarely lost class time during the remaining 180 days of the school year by having to call "time out" to teach manners. I was able to teach instead.

I could probably write another hundred pages about what my students learned from our discussions on manners and the Golden Rule and how it affected our classroom environment, but this chapter is already longer than I intended it to be. In the interest of brevity, let me share with you some of the most important conclusions on which we had consensus:

- Manners and civility have declined because people are more self-centered now, more are influenced by popular culture (particularly the entertainment industry), people try a lot harder these days to be "cool," and there are fewer adult role models who display good manners.

- Society would be much better, and any classroom would be much better, if people treated each other with mutual respect and courtesy.

- Our manners are the way we present ourselves to the world. We're liked or disliked because of our manners. Our reputation is formed by how we treat other people. Manners are important in *all* aspects of life – home, school, sports, business, and any type of social gathering.

- Although many parents are still teaching and modeling good manners in the home, a disappointingly large number of them aren't. If kids aren't learning good manners in the home, they need to learn them somewhere. School seems like the obvious place. It would be a disservice to students to fill their heads with academic information but not help them learn to deal effectively and politely with other people.

> *Good manners offer a lifetime of benefits. Not many*
> *investments boast such a considerable return.*

– Marry Jesse

Good teachers create a caring community

One looks back with appreciation to the brilliant teachers,
but with gratitude to those who touched our human feelings.
The curriculum is so much necessary raw material, but
warmth is the vital element for the growing plant and for
the soul of the child.

— *Carl Jung*

Why kids need to know and care for each other

Posted on the website of The Center for the 4th and 5th R's (Respect and Responsibility) are the 12 principles of a comprehensive approach to Character Education. One of the 12 is "Creating a Caring Classroom Community." Following are the three key ideas presented:

1. Just as children need caring attachments to adults, they also need caring attachments to each other. They are much more likely to accept the values and rules of the group when they feel accepted and affirmed by the group.

2. The peer culture is a powerful moral teacher and influence on student behavior. If teachers do not help to shape a positive peer culture – one that supports the ethical values adults are trying to teach – the peer culture will often develop in the opposite direction, creating peer norms (e.g., cruelty to kids who are different,

disrespect for rules and adult authority) that are antithetical to good character.

3. When students are part of a legitimate caring moral community in the classroom, they learn morality by living it. They receive respect and care, and practice giving it in return. Through daily experiences, respect and care gradually become habits – part of their character.

It all starts with the teacher

Early in my teaching career, I read something by child psychologist Haim Ginott that succinctly summarized and crystallized the role of a teacher in creating a classroom atmosphere. He seemed to capture both my philosophy of teaching and my daily mission, and I wanted to remember what he'd written every time I walked into my classroom. To aid that process I had a friend print it in calligraphy in large letters for me. Then I covered it with clear plastic and taped it to my desk. Every morning when I came into my room, I put down whatever I was carrying, sat down, and read this:

I have come to a frightening conclusion that I am the decisive element in the classroom. It's my personal approach that creates the climate. It's my daily mood that makes the weather. As a teacher, I possess a tremendous power to make a child's life miserable or joyous. I can be a tool of torture or an instrument of inspiration. I can humiliate or humor, hurt or heal. In all situations, it is <u>my</u> response that decides whether a crisis will be escalated or deescalated and a child humanized or dehumanized.

This is a well-known piece in educational circles. I've heard many speakers quote it, and I've seen it in many books and other sources. I've also shared it with literally thousands of teachers across the country; it's a vital part of many of my presentations about teaching strategies. I think every teacher should not only read it, but etch it in their hearts and put it into practice every day of their teaching careers.

Before I leave this incredible pearl of wisdom about the influence of a teacher, I want to zero in on a few of his key words. Please note that Ginott writes, "It's my *personal* approach that creates the climate." He didn't say anything about the college he attended, his degrees, or any other academic credentials. Nor did he say anything about his teaching experience, his knowledge, or his research and publications. It's because none of them have anything to do with the climate in his classroom. But his *personal* approach – how he treats his students – has everything to do with the climate. Kids don't care how much you know until they know how much you care.

The other word I want to zero in on is *inspiration*. "You can be a tool of torture or an instrument of inspiration." This is one of the most powerful words in the dictionary and one of the most important responsibilities of a teacher – to inspire his or her students. It means to awaken them, to help them discover the possibilities in their lives, to bring out the best in them. This may sound corny or excessively idealistic, but it's straight from this author's heart. Passionate teachers inspire their students.

> *The mediocre teacher tells.*
> *The good teacher explains.*
> *The superior teacher demonstrates.*
> *The great teacher inspires.*
>   – William Arthur Ward

When both the teacher and the students care

The best teachers show, right from the beginning, how much they care for their students. But they do more than that. They help their students get to know each other, understand each other, and ultimately care for each other. It does wonders for the classroom atmosphere. It always amazed me when students told me that I was the only teacher they had who set up ways for them to bond with each other early in the year. Many of them told me that they could go through an entire school year in a class and only know the names of a few other students. The former athlete in me always thought, "That's like being on a team and not knowing the names of your teammates."

Students have two common goals that they can help each other attain. The first is to learn the subject matter of a course. The second is to learn good social skills while growing as a person. Please notice that I said they *can* help each other. That means they're *able* to help each other. But it doesn't mean that it will happen naturally. It's the teacher's responsibility to create opportunities in the first few days of school for students to develop healthy and supportive relationships with each other.

In the previous two chapters I explained a couple of the most important things I did as a teacher. The first was to individually welcome each student into my class every day of the year. The second was to teach manners and the Golden Rule on the first day of school. These two strategies went a long way in letting the kids know, early on, what type of atmosphere I hoped for in the class. They also learned that I couldn't do it alone. I needed their cooperation in establishing the best possible environment for teaching and learning.

The Two-Minute Interview

One of the simplest and most engaging activities I ever used with my students was what became known as "The Two-Minute Interview." Like many of my strategies, it started out as a good idea that didn't work very effectively. After tweaking it a few times, I finally got it right. Initially, I gave my students some time at the beginning of the year to interview each other and to learn five interesting things about each of their classmates. It didn't work for a couple of reasons. One is that it was too vague. Students didn't know what kinds of questions they should ask. That led to the next problem – it took too long. So after some trial and error (a lot of error), I finally came up with this simple page:

THE TWO-MINUTE INTERVIEW

Live with – Own – Place – Goal – Achievement –
Hobby – Special interest – Hero – Other

Name _____

1) _____
2) _____
3) _____
4) _____
5) _____

Name _____

1) _____
2) _____
3) _____
4) _____
5) _____

Name _____

1) _____
2) _____
3) _____
4) _____
5) _____

Name _____

1) _____
2) _____
3) _____
4) _____
5) _____

Name _____

1) _____
2) _____
3) _____
4) _____
5) _____

Name _____

1) _____
2) _____
3) _____
4) _____
5) _____

Name _____

1) _____
2) _____
3) _____
4) _____
5) _____

Name _____

1) _____
2) _____
3) _____
4) _____
5) _____

Name _____

1) _____
2) _____
3) _____
4) _____
5) _____

Name _____

1) _____
2) _____
3) _____
4) _____
5) _____

The Two-Minute Interview Explained

Instructions: Each student was required to interview all the other students in the class on a one-to-one basis. They were given some class time for the first five days of school, and they were on their own to finish it within three weeks. When they came into class, they paired up with someone and did their interviews. They were required to turn it in, and they received grade points for it like any other assignment.

Trigger words and questions:

Live with – With whom do you live? You may include siblings away at college.

Own – What is something you own that is very special to you? Why?

Place – What is the best place you've ever been? Or is there a place you'd like to visit?

Goal – What's an important goal you have for your life?

Achievement – What's your proudest achievement thus far?

Hobby – Do you have one? If yes, what is it?

Special interest – Do you have a special interest in a subject or activity? Explain.

Hero – Who is someone you greatly admire? Why? It must be someone you know.

Other – Ask a question of your choice. It must be better than "What's your sign?"

Format:

On The Two-Minute Interview page in this book, I have two columns of five, so you could do 10 interviews on one side and 10 more on the other side if the page was copied back-to-back. But if your classes are larger than 20, you can simply space out the page differently. I always had large classes. My Two-Minute Interview page had three columns of six. A student could conduct 18 interviews on each side for a total of 36 in a particularly large class.

Student response:

My students loved this simple activity/assignment. They said it was fun and that it helped them get to know some interesting things about their classmate and their teacher quickly and easily. They were required to conduct one of the two-minute interviews with me, and I interviewed each of them as well. After three weeks we all knew each other well.

Making students feel that they count

We all need to feel important, that we matter,
that we are noticed.

– Marilyn Gootman and Larry Whipple
The Caring Teacher's Guide to Discipline

Way back in 1936, Dale Carnegie published one of the most practical and readable books on human relations ever written. It's called *How To Win Friends And Influence People*, and at last count it had sold more than 16 million copies. It continues to sell today at the rate of about 250,000 per year. Carnegie, though not a trained psychologist, had a profound understanding of human nature, particularly in regard to the basic needs of people. One of those needs is the desire to feel as though we matter, that we count for something. It doesn't make any difference if we're in pre-kindergarten, attending college, or enjoying our retirement. We want to feel that our lives have meaning.

Carnegie says if you understand this need, what he calls an "unfaltering human hunger," and you can satisfy it in others, you'll hold people in the palm of your hand. He writes that "even the undertaker will be sorry" when you die. To make his point he quotes a great philosopher and educator, as well as a renowned psychologist.

The deepest urge in human nature is the desire
to feel important.
– John Dewey

The deepest principle in human nature is the
craving to be appreciated.
– William James

One of the simple ways we can fulfill this need in our students is to let them know that we're interested in them. We can do this by asking questions about their lives, about their families, and about what's important to them. I did this with a personal-information sheet that they loved to fill out – simply because it was about them!

Period_____   Name _____

Who are you?

We're going to spend a lot of time together this year, so I'd like to get to know you, not only as a student, but also as a person. Please answer the following questions to help me in this process. Feel free to ignore any questions you choose. All of your answers will remain private. Feel free to ask me any of the same questions.

1. What is your favorite leisure-time activity? _____

2. What is something you do well? _____

3. What would you like to do in your career? _____

4. Do you plan to attend college?   YES   NO

5. If yes, which one would be your first choice? _____

6. Do you like school?   YES   NO
Briefly explain: _____

7. What do like the most about school?   _____

8. What do you like the least about school? _____

9. What two words best describe you as a student? _____

10 What two words best describe you as a person? _____

11. Where were you born? _____

12. How many of the 50 states have you been in? _____

13. How many foreign countries have you been in? _____

14. If you could go anywhere in the U.S., where would it be? _____

15. If you could go anywhere in the world, where would it be? _____

16. If you could meet any living person, who would it be? _____
Why? _____

17. What are three things you'd like to achieve in your lifetime? _____
_____

18. Who is the best person you've ever known? _____
Why is he/she the best? _____

19. What are some of the things you're most thankful for? _____
_____

20. What is your best quality? _____

21. What's your favorite subject in school? _____

22. Who's the best teacher you've ever had? _____

Why was he/she the best? _____

_____

23. Who's your best friend? _____

Why? _____

_____

24. What is a valuable lesson you've learned about life? _____

_____

25. What is something you'd like to learn to do? _____

26. What extra-curricular activities are you involved in at school? _____

_____

27. What activities are you involved in outside of school, including your job? _____

_____

28. What's your favorite sport? _____

29. Who's your favorite athlete? _____

30. What's your favorite team? _____

31. What's your favorite TV program? _____

32. What's the best movie you've ever seen? _____

33. Who's your favorite actor? _____

34. Who's your favorite actress? _____

35. What's the best book you've ever read? _____

36. If you could own any car, what would it be? _____

37. What's your favorite type of music? _____

38. Who is your favorite male recording artist?_____

39. Who is your favorite female recording artist? _____

40. Is there anything else you'd like me to know about you? If yes, please explain below

_____

_____

_____

_____

_____

_____

_____

_____

FAQs regarding the personal-information sheet

When did I hand it out?

During the first week of school, usually the third or fourth day.

Was it done in class or as a homework assignment?

I've done both, but I found that it worked better as a homework assignment. This saved me class time because I had so much I wanted to cover in the first two weeks of school. It was probably one of the most popular homework assignments I ever gave. It was all about them.

How did you use the information?

First of all, I copied the two pages back-to-back so all the information would be on one sheet of paper. Then I filed them alphabetically in one folder per class. I read all of them over a period of about three weeks. This information, along with that obtained during The Two–Minute Interview, gave me a pretty good idea of what my students were all about. I often used it to ask them questions or start a conversation when I was greeting them at the door. They always lit up because it showed them I was interested in them.

Seating arrangements and the "No Cliques" policy

Many teachers assign seats alphabetically on the first day of school. Others allow the students to sit anywhere they want. I did neither. You never know what you're going to end up with when you do it alphabetically, and letting them sit where they want is encouraging the formation of cliques. It works against the creation of a caring community. I allowed them to sit where they wanted on the first day of school. That way I would find out early where they should *not* be sitting. I told them to not get too comfortable because as soon as I learned all their names (about three days) it would be "musical chairs" for the rest of the year. They would be on the move each day, sitting next to and around different students. All the desks were numbered randomly, and each student went to the next highest number the following day. See the next page.

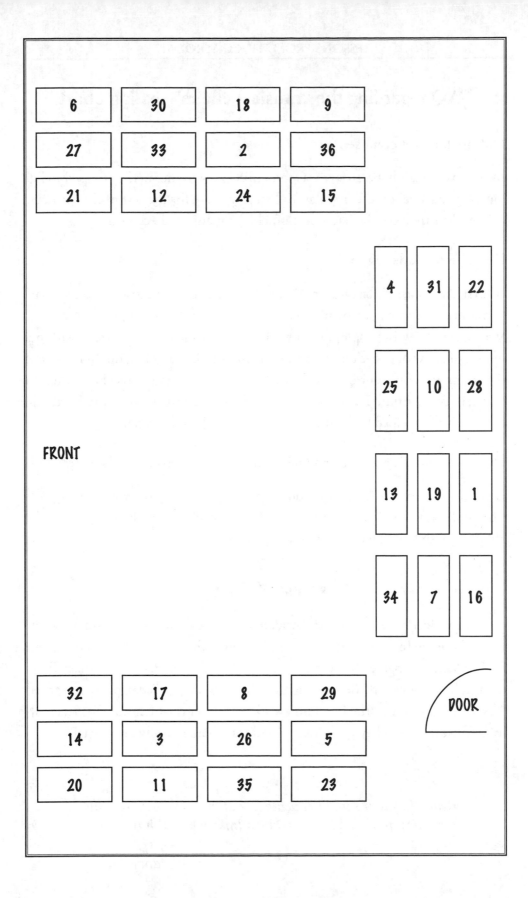

FAQ regarding the "musical chairs" seating chart

Did the kids get confused?

At first, yes. Mainly because it was something new to them. They're used to being assigned seats on the first day and staying there for the rest of the semester or year. But they got the hang of it quickly and adjusted accordingly.

How did the kids respond?

At first they resisted for two simple reasons. The first is that we're "territorial" by nature. We want our own space. Secondly, we're also "cliquey" by nature. We want to be with people we know. But they warmed up to the idea within a matter of a few days because they saw the merits of sitting in a different part of the room with different classmates each day. It also made it easier for them to do their Two-Minute Interviews. Many of the students thanked me for doing this because it helped bring the class together early in the year.

How did your Guest Teachers (substitutes) know who the kids were?

Early in the year I gave every student an assigned seat for when I was gone from class. I had a seating chart for my Guest Teacher to make it easier to take attendance so he/she would know who was sitting where.

First test of the year

As an added incentive for my students to learn about their classmates early, I told them the first test of the year would require them to identify each student by first and last name (both spelled correctly) and one fact from their Two–Minute Interview with that classmate. More than 90 percent of them earned A's on this test and on the first homework assignment, which was the personal-information sheet. They got off to a good start academically and socially.

Real education should educate us out of self into something far finer; into a selflessness which links with all humanity.

– Nancy Astor

Good teachers protect the atmosphere from toxic words

Poorly chosen words can stifle enthusiasm, dampen spirits, and be both offensive and hurtful. In short, they can poison the atmosphere.

– Professor Erwin G. Hall

The power of words

If we made a list of all the things we underestimate, words could well be at the top. We seem to take them for granted because they've been our main tools of communication since we were about two years old. As a result, we often blurt things out without thinking about the impact our words might have on others, on ourselves, and on the atmosphere surrounding us. Parents and teachers, more than anyone, should constantly remind themselves that their words – and the way they say them – have enormous power in shaping the lives of children. In addition to choosing our own words carefully, we need to help kids grow in awareness of the power of their words.

Choosing an atmosphere

After the first day of class, my students had a pretty good understanding of the type of environment I was trying to create (with their help) in my classroom. Greeting them at the door and spending 30 or more minutes on manners and the Golden Rule went a long way in helping us get off to a good start. On the second day, after welcoming them at the door and taking attendance, I started class with a quick vocabulary lesson. I wrote two words on the board in large letters:

TOXIC   NOURISHING

I asked them if they knew the meaning of these two words. It won't surprise you that some of the kids knew both words, some knew one word, and a few didn't know either. We defined and discussed both so everyone would know what I was talking about. It's a common mistake for teachers, especially in high school, to assume that kids always know the meaning of the words that they're using. Remembering my own limited vocabulary at that age, I always clarified terms before we went further into the lesson. We agreed on the following synonyms for the two key terms:

TOXIC – poisonous, contaminated, lethal

NOURISHING – healthful, beneficial, wholesome

Next came a question. It may seem like a no-brainer, but there was a method to my madness. I asked them, "Which type of atmosphere do you want – toxic or nourishing?" They all chose nourishing, and a few wondered out loud why I would even ask. They often asked, "Has anyone ever chosen toxic?" I told them yes, and that my point in asking the question was to remind them that we do, indeed, *choose* our atmosphere. I told them that in my early years of teaching, before I learned how to deal with it, I had a few classes choose a toxic atmosphere without even realizing they were making a choice.

This was a little confusing to them because, as I'll explain more fully in Chapter 14, students are often unaware of the choices they're presented with on a daily basis.

Now I had my main question of the day set up. Here it is: "If we all want a nourishing atmosphere, then would you agree with me that it would be bad for the class if we allowed anyone to spray poison in the room?" This usually resulted in some puzzled looks and the occasional, "Huh?" The reason is simple: Kids tend to be much more literal than adults. They would ask, "Why would anyone want to spray poison in a classroom?" I think some of them actually visualized someone coming into class with a big can of poison spray and letting it rip. My response to their question was (with a big smile), "The sad truth is that both students and teachers have been spraying poison into classrooms – sometimes in mega-doses – since schools began." More puzzled looks.

Words as poison – complete with a visual aid

I explained that certain types of words can be toxic. Some can be hurtful and offensive. Others can be gross and disgusting. Some words can evoke anger or sadness. Others can be rude and disrespectful. And they can drag us down by casting a negative pall around us. Spewing these kinds of toxic words, whether it be in a classroom, a home, a business, or at a social gathering, is like spraying verbal poison into the atmosphere.

I held up an empty can of Lysol bathroom deodorant that had been doctored a bit. I'd drawn a skull and crossbones on a piece of paper, written "poison" underneath it, and wrapped it around the can. It now looked like a can of poison spray. I told the kids that I'd leave it in the front of the room, either on my desk or on the tray of the chalkboard, as a reminder to all of us to not spray verbal poison into the classroom. I also told them that when someone slipped and let out a little poison, I'd hold up the can and say, "Oops ... we've had a little seepage." No one wanted to be the cause of that happening. I learned early in my career that catchy phrases and visual aids always helped kids remember concepts more clearly and for a longer period of time. I used them whenever I could.

Now that my students grasped the concept of "verbal poison," I wanted to make it more specific. I went back to the board and pointed to the word "TOXIC."

I asked them, "What are the types of things people say that poison the atmosphere – the types of things you don't like to hear?" I suggested that we make a list of them. Brainstorming together, we came up with far more categories that I had originally thought there were. I was thinking there would probably be about a dozen of them, and we could call them the "Dirty Dozen." But we came up with 30, and they naturally became known as...

The Dirty Thirty

These have been published in two of my previous books – *Positive Words, Powerful Results* and *The 10 Commandments of Common Sense* – but I don't want to be accused of being a shameless promoter by writing, "If you want to see the list, you'll just have to go out and buy one of those books." So here they are:

1. Bragging
2. Swearing and other gross-out language
3. Gossip (especially the vicious kind)
4. Angry words
5. Lies
6. Mean-spirited and hurtful words
7. Judgmental words
8. Playing "poor me" – the self-pity game
9. Making discouraging remarks
10. Embarrassing and/or humiliating others
11. Excessive fault-finding and criticism
12. Complaining, whining, moaning, groaning
13. Rude and inconsiderate language
14. Teasing
15. Using words to manipulate others
16. Phony and insincere compliments, flattery
17. Ethnic and racial slurs
18. Sexist comments

19. Age-related put-downs (one of my contributions to the list)
20. Being negative – always pointing out what's wrong
21. Threats
22. Arguing
23. Interrupting – not letting the other person finish
24. Playing "trump" – always topping someone else's story
25. Being a know-it-all
26. Sarcasm
27. Yelling, screaming
28. Talking down to people – being condescending
29. Exaggerating, blowing things out of proportion
30. Blaming and accusing others

The Flagrant Five

Since we ended up with a much longer list that I'd originally imagined, I was curious as to which ones my students heard most often and which ones were the most offensive. Although they disliked the entire Dirty Thirty, five of them seemed to keep coming up as both the most frequent and most foul. Here they are:

1. Swearing and other offensive words
2. Complaining, whining, moaning, groaning
3. Put-downs – mean-spirited and hurtful words
4. Rude and inconsiderate language
5. Gossip (especially the vicious kind)

The swearing issue

There was general agreement that four of the Flagrant Five were self-explanatory. But there was some confusion and disagreement on the first category – swearing and other offensive words. To begin with, the kids growing up since the early 80s don't remember a time when there *wasn't* a lot of swearing and other gross terms. This kind of language has been a major part of the culture throughout their lifetimes. What's swearing to many adults is just everyday language to many of our students. Many of them aren't even slightly offended by words that older adults find totally abhorrent. This makes the issue tricky for schools and teachers, especially because language that's now used in many homes is not acceptable at school. Let me share with you some of the strategies I developed for dealing with this very sticky problem.

Strategy #1 – Emphasize courtesy and a professional level of language

I didn't want my students to think I was a prude, a bluenose, or a right-wing religious zealot, so I explained that I was simply trying to maintain high professional standards. After all, education *is* a profession. I asked them a series of questions that always made the point and always provoked both thought and some excellent discussions:

- Would you think differently of me if I constantly used swear words while teaching? What if every day I began class by saying, "Get your f---ing binders out and let's get started"?

- Would it lower the standards and damage the atmosphere in the class?

- Do educated and cultured people use this type of language?

- Do people in positions of leadership (government, business, education) use this type of language?

- Are there places in our society in which you don't want to hear these types of words?

- Do you think some people might be offended when they hear these types of words?

- Are people who frequently use foul language in public rude or polite?

Strategy #2 – Ask your students what people who swear frequently reveal about themselves

This question, especially after answering the ones above, was the one that stirred up the most interest and resulted in the best discussion. Many of the kids said they'd never really thought about how their swearing was affecting other people, and at the same time, revealing some not-so-good things about themselves. Here are their conclusions about people (including themselves) who swear frequently:

1. They're angry

2. They're uneducated, uncouth, or both.

3. They're inconsiderate of other people.

4. They have limited vocabularies.

5. They're trying hard to be "cool."

6. Swearing has become a bad habit for them.

7. They lack imagination and creativity.

8. They can't think for themselves. They just repeat what they hear.

9. They have filthy minds.

10. They have no class. They're clueless

When I did this for the first time in the early 80s, Jessica, a junior in my U.S. History class, stayed after to talk to me about it. She said, "I'm really glad we did this. I'm embarrassed to say that I swear *way* too much, and it *has* become a habit. Now that I know I'm saying a lot of things about myself every time I swear, I have some incentive to clean up my language." Over the next 20 years, I heard many similar comments.

Strategy #3 – Be specific

"Swearing" is both a general and a vague term. As I stated earlier, the word means different things to people of different generations. For instance, when it first became a problem in the early 80s, I simply asked my students at the beginning of the year to honor my policy of no swearing in the classroom. No problem. A day later a student somewhat loudly announced to a group of his friends that he felt like "s---." I gave him a rather surprised look, smiled, and asked, "Don't you remember that we all agreed yesterday that we wouldn't swear in class?" He looked at me with an even more surprised look and said with all sincerity, "I didn't swear." We needed to determine what *was* and what *was not* swearing.

I wrote a large letter "F" on the board. I said, "This is the first letter of a famous four-letter word that's slang for sexual intercourse. Does everyone know what word I mean?" They all did. Then I asked, "How many of you think it's a swear word?" About two-thirds of them did and the other third didn't. I told them, "It's a swear word to me, so I'd appreciate it if you wouldn't use it in class." Then I put a large "S" on the board, and we went through a similar process to establish it as an official swear word.

When I put the letter "B" on the board, they immediately asked, "Which one?" My response was, "Both of them."

I asked them if there were other words they had questions about, because it was important for us to have a mutual understanding and agreement. The kids had questions and observations. One of the observations was that many of the words I consider to be swear words are used on network television during the traditional family hour of 8-9 p.m. The two "B" words – bitch and bastard – were among them. I acknowledged that I'd heard them myself, but had a clear idea of what I considered to be swear words, even if some of their parents didn't.

Strategy #4 – Eliminate other offensive words

I asked my students if there were any words they found even more offensive than the traditional swear words. They all said yes, so I suggested that we spell them all out. Here's what we eliminated:

- All derogatory references to race.

- All derogatory references to intelligence or lack thereof.

- All derogatory references to sexual preference.

- All derogatory references to a person's physical appearance.

- "That sucks" – "That bites" – "That blows" (popular terms, but crude).

- "Pissed off" – One of my students said it was better than being "pissed on," but it was still unacceptable.

- "Shut up" and "Shut your face." Younger students usually use these. I told them these phrases were "tacky," and one of the reasons for getting an education is to develop a more sophisticated vocabulary. I suggested that instead of saying "Shut up!" they might want to try, "I would appreciate it if you would refrain from speaking in that manner." This suggestion always got a laugh, and many of my students had a lot of fun using this new phrase.

The most important thing to remember when discussing this challenging subject with students is the manner in which you do it. As I stated earlier, tone of voice and body language are a big part of our communication. Threats of punishment are ineffective. Condemning all swear words doesn't work, either. What's far more effective is stressing that there's a time and a place for everything, and that the classroom isn't one of those times or places in which to use offensive language. Also effective is stressing the influence that language has on the atmosphere of the class. Toxic or nourishing?

Did I get every kid to conclude that all swearing is wrong? Did I get all my students to stop swearing forever? No. But I did make some valuable points with them regarding the impact language has on us, what it reveals about ourselves, and how it affects the atmosphere, no matter where we are. And it virtually eliminated toxic words in the atmosphere of my class.

A few friendly reminders

The world does not require so much to be informed as to be reminded.

– Hannah More
Teacher, 1745-1833

I'm a strong believer in the power of visible reminders. There'll be more about their importance in Chapter 11. So far, I've only shared one – the Lysol can that I turned into a symbol of spraying poison into the room. I added a few others on the day we talked about toxic words. After we wrote and discussed the Dirty Thirty and the Flagrant Five, I told my students that on the following day there would be six new signs in the room. The wall to my right was colorfully decorated with posters of natural wonders and people participating in fun and adventurous activities. Also on that wall was the clock, about eight feet up. I had deliberately left some space around it so I could put the six new signs there. I figured they'd get looked at frequently. Here's what they saw: (see illustration on following page)

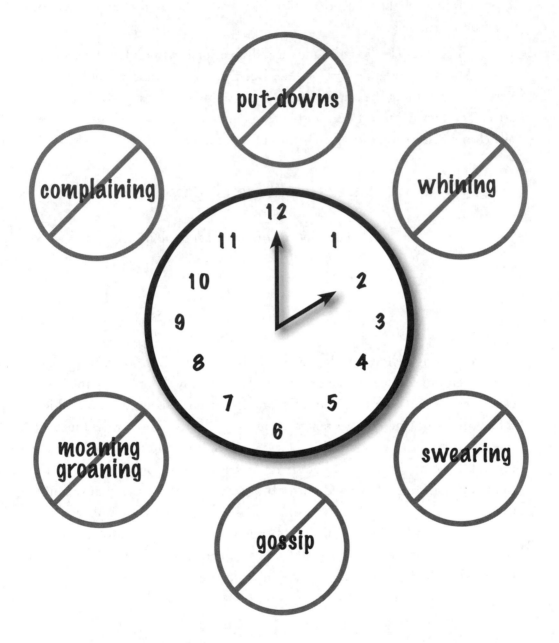

Two ways that kids innocently, yet frequently, poison the atmosphere
And how to solve the problem in a fun way

I want to discuss the two most common examples of students of all ages poisoning the atmosphere of a classroom without even knowing they're doing it. I'm convinced they're universal, and teachers everywhere I go agree. It will be more difficult to explain them in writing because I can't add voice inflection and body language as I do when presenting in person. But I'm confident that you'll understand my point.

1. "Do we *have* to ... ?"

On an average day in all schools across the country (and probably around the globe), students begin a question with these four words. While I have no research to back it up, it's my contention that this happens more than a million times a day. Let's say the question is, "Do we have to do homework tonight?" The real emphasis is placed on the first four words. They don't ask this question with smiles on their faces and in pleasant tones of voice. Instead, they have pained looks on their faces, and the question is asked in an ugly and whiny tone of voice. It sounds worse than scraping your fingernails on the chalkboard. It happens almost daily, yet teachers rarely attempt to deal with it.

I found a way to virtually eliminate it early in the year in a way that was fun for both the students and myself. Someone asks, "Do we have to ... ?" in the usual whiny voice. I react in mock horror, call time out by forming a "T" with my hands like a basketball referee, hold up my can of poison spray, and say (with a big smile), "Ooh, we just had a little accident. Someone let some poison into the room. But it's OK. It's early in the year, and these things will happen. Let's make sure we fix it now so it won't happen again." I then go over to the area of the clock and point to the "no complaining, no whining, no moaning or groaning" signs.

Then I say, "Here's how we fix it. First, we're going to change one little word in the question. We're going to change *have* to *get*. Then we're going to change the whiny tone of voice into a pleasant tone and the negative body language into positive body language." Then I demonstrate how the question should be asked. I put a big smile on my face, and in an excited tone of voice, I ask, "Mr. Urban, do we *get* to do homework tonight?" It never fails to make them laugh. I ask if someone wants to try it, someone does, and the class gets another laugh. I also tell them that there are so many benefits to doing homework that they should be *begging* me for it every night.

2. "Oh, no."

The two words above look short and innocent. But teachers know otherwise. They can both be very long and deadly to the atmosphere of a class. When I hand out a sheet of paper early in the year, students have a conditioned response stronger than the one Pavlov's dog had. They think work is coming – as in reading, writing, or even worse, thinking – and they respond by making each of those two little words above last for about 10 seconds (as in, "Oooooooooooooooh, noooooooooooooooo!") while uttering them in the whiniest and most deadly tone possible.

Again, I react in mock horror, call time out by forming a "T," hold up the can of poison spray, and say (with a big smile), "Ooh, we just had another little accident. Someone let some poison into the room. But it's OK. It's early in the year, and these things will happen. Let's make sure we fix it now so it won't happen again." Then I go over to the clock area and again point to the signs.

Then I do the best selling job I can in regard to my handouts. I tell them they're far more interesting than a textbook, easier to read, easier to understand, and get to the point a lot more quickly. Then I demonstrate how we fix the problem and eliminate the poisonous and elongated "Oooooooooooooooh, noooooooooooooooo!" When I hand out a paper, I tell them, I'd like the first student who receives it to look at it excitedly and say with an equally excited tone of voice, "Oh boy! This looks like it will be a wonderful learning experience!" They break out in laughter. I ask if anyone wants to try it. Someone does. I give her the sheet of paper, she exclaims how excited she is to receive it and what a fabulous learning experience it will be, and we all laugh again. The poison is gone. I tell them my handouts are so good they should be cheering when they get them, not moaning. I actually enjoyed handing out papers and often preface it with, "Oh, you guys are going to love this one. Who wants the first copy?"

Two famous authors on the power of words

There's one other simple exercise I did with my students regarding the power of words. It always evoked meaningful discussion and resulted in a deeper understanding of the impact of negative words. I used quotations from two well-known authors. The first is Robert Fulghum, author of the best-selling book *All I Ever Needed To Know I Learned in Kindergarten*. Most of us learned a familiar saying when we were children, usually right after another child said something that hurt our feelings. It goes like this: "Sticks and stones can break my bones, but words can never hurt me." Unfortunately, it's not true. Words can hurt a lot more than sticks and stones. Fulghum has a more accurate version of it.

> *Sticks and stones can break my bones, but words*
> *can break my heart.*
> *– Robert Fulghum*

Here's the second one by Maya Angelou, the Pulitzer Prize-winning author and poet:

> *Words go into the body. So they can cause us to be*
> *well and hopeful and happy and high-energy and*
> *wondrous and funny and cheerful. Or they can*
> *cause us to be depressed. They get into the body*
> *and cause us to be sullen and sour and depressed*
> *and, finally, sick.*
> *– Maya Angelou*

All I did was copy those two quotations onto a handout, leave some space under each, and type these words: "Please respond." My students had plenty to write, and even more to say in the discussion that followed.

All together, these activities and strategies went a long way in removing the toxic words from my classroom. I don't think we ever succeeded at the 100 percent level, but 98 percent is still a strong A, and we achieved that mark regularly.

Cleaning up the most toxic place on campus

I can't leave this topic without sharing one more important story about toxic words. It has to do with my collection of signs that have the red circles with the slashes through them, as in "no complaining," "no whining," etc. In 1998, when I was still teaching full time, I went to Minnesota to speak to all the teachers of a large suburban school district. Among other topics, I spoke about the harmful effects of toxic words, how I dealt with the issue in my own classroom, and then showed the signs to everyone. After I finished speaking several teachers came up to the stage to discuss some of my topics in more detail. One of them was an English teacher at a high school in the district. He asked me if he could look through my signs, and I told him to go right ahead.

A few minutes later he picked up two of the signs, held them up with their backs showing (so I didn't know which ones they were), and said he had an idea he'd like to share with me. I'm always open to ideas from teachers, so I said, "I'm listening." He asked, "How would you like to do something to improve every faculty in the country and make a lot of money at the same time?" I said, "It sounds too good to be true, so it probably is, but what's your idea?" He said, "Take these two signs, make them ten times bigger than they are, and post them in every faculty lounge in the country." Then he turned them around so I could see that they were the "no complaining" and the "no gossip" signs.

Sadly, this is true in too many workrooms and lounges in schools throughout the country. Those rooms are often the most toxic places on campus. When I share this story with audiences comprised of mostly teachers, I always get a strong reaction. Sometimes they applaud, they nod their heads up and down, they laugh, and I often hear someone yell out "Right on!" or "Let's do it!" Who do teachers complain about? Kids and administrators. Who do they gossip about? Anyone who's not there that day. It was about three weeks into my first year of teaching when I figured out that the lounge wasn't the place I wanted to eat lunch. I never ate lunch there for the remainder of my career. And I'm sure I was gossiped about.

If we're going to be proactive in our attempts to significantly reduce the effects of toxic words on campus and in the classroom, we need to start with the staff. By that I mean every person who works at the school. Adults as well as kids need to be occasionally reminded about the impact their words can have on the school environment. There are a number of simple solutions to this problem. Here are two of them:

One school I spoke at did exactly what the Minnesota teacher suggested. They enlarged the two signs and posted them in the teachers' lounge. Even though I never made a penny from it, I was delighted to learn that it had a positive effect. A teacher at the school sent an e-mail three weeks later to tell me, "The lounge is so much more pleasant now. No one wants to complain or gossip with those two big signs staring them in the face. And best of all, the four biggest gossips in the school now eat lunch somewhere else – probably so they can gossip. Thank you for bringing your signs."

At another school the staff wrote up a "Code of Professional Conduct" during workshops in late August, just before classes began. It had several parts to it, and each member of the staff signed it. Some of the sections in it went beyond the use of toxic words, but these two did appear in it: "I will do my part in promoting a pleasant atmosphere in all places on campus where we congregate," and "In teaching our students about the harmful effects of toxic words, I'll do my best to practice what I preach."

Let's make our homes and schools better places. We can start by banning all toxic verbal weapons.

– L. Harry Goldman

Good teachers nourish the atmosphere with kind and affirming words

When words are both true and kind, they can change our world.

– Buddha

Replacing the toxic words

The previous chapter was devoted to sharing my strategies for eliminating toxic words from the classroom atmosphere. This chapter deals exclusively with my strategies for replacing them – for nourishing the atmosphere with positive words and teaching my students to do the same.

After we completed the lists of the Dirty Thirty and the Flagrant Five, discussed them, covered the topics of swearing and put-downs at length, brought out the famous poison spray can, and posted the six signs that reminded us to not spew toxins into the atmosphere, we moved to the second word on the board – **NOURISHING**. Keep in mind that we defined it as healthful, beneficial, and wholesome. It's a good thing to remove the negatives from the atmosphere. It's an even better thing to replace them with positives. I went to the board, pointed to **NOURISHING**, and asked my students to tell me the types of words most people actually *like* to hear. Again, we came up with 30, so they also had to have a nickname. We called them ...

The Thoughtful Thirty

1. Give encouragement
2. Express thanks
3. Acknowledge others
4. Extend greetings
5. Give a compliment
6. Congratulate someone
7. Teach, give instruction
8. Offer words of comfort
9. Inspire others
10. Celebrate and cheer
11. Inquire, express interest
12. Mend relationships
13. Make others laugh
14. Show faith and trust
15. Share good news
16. Praise, honor, build up
17. Express caring
18. Show understanding and empathy
19. Give approval
20. Extend an invitation
21. Show courtesy and respect
22. Give helpful advice
23. Apologize
24. Forgive
25. Offer to help
26. Tell the truth
27. Point out the good
28. Use terms of affection
29. Supply needed information
30. Communicate love

Teaching kids to build up instead of tear down

Be positive with people and you'll get positive results.
– Ken Blanchard

My students didn't have any difficulty understanding that put-downs can cause deep and long-lasting pain. Mainly because they'd all experienced it. Most of them were delighted that I brought up the subject on the second day of school, and they were even more delighted to learn that they were in a class in which put-downs wouldn't be allowed. Getting them to agree on a "No Put-Downs" policy was the easy part.

Teaching them to do the opposite – to build up, to praise, to compliment, to affirm, to bring out the best in one another – was the hard part. In fact, I would say it was one of the most challenging tasks I ever took on as a teacher, especially in the early days. But it was worth all of the initial frustrations, and it was worth every minute we ever spent on it. I would even go so far as to say that teaching kids to build up instead of tear down was one of the most valuable and powerful concepts I ever taught.

It all started with a friend and colleague. I've mentioned Tim Hansel in a few of my previous books. The reason is simple: he's the ultimate life-enhancer, and he had a profound impact on my life. It was from him that I first learned how powerful positive words can be. As Buddha says in the quotation opening this chapter, "When words are both true and kind, they can change our world." Tim's words changed *my* world, and what he taught me has been changing other peoples' worlds since the early 1970s.

The famous motivational speaker from Texas, Zig Ziglar, has several wonderful phrases. One of them is, "Be a good finder!" He adds that we usually find what we're looking for, and that if we look for the good in life, in the world, and in other people, we'll probably find it. Tim was the best "good finder" I've ever known. But he took Ziglar a step further. He not only *looked* for the good and *found* the good, he *celebrated* the good. Instead of complaining, criticizing, gossiping, or swearing, Tim always had something good to say. He nourished the atmosphere wherever he went.

He was particularly good at affirming people, whether it was a student or a colleague. If he found a quality in you that he liked and admired, he would tell you directly. Very few people are comfortable doing this. One of his favorite questions was, "Do you know what I like the most about you?" Believe me, everyone wants to know the answer. Tim was like a ray of sunshine. He brightened the lives of everyone around him. And he was especially good at bringing out the best in his students.

Since kids are so prone to putting each other down, I couldn't help wondering if they could actually be taught to do the opposite – to recognize each other in positive ways, to build on the good in one another. I had to give it a try. So I had a discussion one afternoon with my 12th-grade Psychology students. They were wonderful kids who were all in the class by choice, since it was an elective. I told them they were a terrific class – motivated, polite, hardworking, and excellent in discussions – but that I felt a need to discuss one area of concern. When they asked me what it was, I responded, "I know it's a pretty routine thing around campus, but I think you put each other down too much." Here were their observations, and my response to each of them:

- "It's just what kids do." – "I'm well aware that it's what kids do, but that doesn't make it OK."

- "We're just kidding." – "I'm not so sure I buy into that. You may act like you're kidding, and even say, 'Just kidding,' but you still get your zinger in."

- "We don't do it during class time." – "No, you don't, but you do it out in the hallway on the way in, and you do it in the room before class starts. It remains in the atmosphere."

- "Nobody gets hurt by it." – "That's probably true some of the time, but I think when most kids get teased or put down in front of their classmates, they're either embarrassed, hurt, or both."

We ended up having a lengthy discussion about the issue. And most of them did admit to a couple of things. First, there were way too many put-downs at school, and that it had been going on since the early grades. Rarely did anyone do anything about it. Second, many of the kids did admit to often being stung by other students' cutting remarks, whether they were kidding or not. They also agreed that if they got put down in the hallway just before class started, the hurt would carry over into class time. So our "No Put-Downs" policy was extended to the hallway and the room even before class started.

It was at this point that I decided to go for it. I suggested that we replace the put-down language with affirming language. "What's that?" was the first question. I said, "It's the opposite of putting someone down. It's building someone up. It's finding the good in another person and letting him or her know what you found." Right after I said this, the room went stone-cold silent. They stared at me like I was from outer space. The looks on their faces seemed to be asking, "You mean you're actually suggesting that we say complimentary things instead of pimping (that was the word being used at the time) on each other?" Then, after a few moments of silence, one of the students did voice an opinion. He said, "Oh man, that would be awkward." Then one of his classmates chimed in with, "Yeah, it would be embarrassing, too."

At this point I smiled and said, "OK, let's talk about *why* saying something nice to another person would be awkward and embarrassing." The answer was simple: It was something they just didn't do. My point was that it's almost always a little awkward or embarrassing in the early stages of learning anything new. I used the examples of dancing, riding a two-wheel bike, throwing or catching a ball, snow skiing, water skiing, skate boarding, even driving a car. I said, "Even when you're learning to do something positive, you usually have to work your way through the awkward, embarrassing stage so you can get to a place where the new skill feels comfortable and natural." I asked them if they were willing to give it a try, even if it felt uncomfortable at the beginning. They assured me they would, and we agreed to start the next day. But it was delayed for one day.

A lesson in life from a service for the dead

If you've heard me speak, there's a good chance you know this story. I've told it hundreds of times because it so effectively makes an important point about affirming language. If you've read my second book, *Positive Words, Powerful Results,* you've read this story before. I'm telling it again for those who haven't heard it or read it before. It's one of my favorites.

The day after my students agreed to give affirming language a try, I was absent from class. I taught my four morning classes, but I had to have another teacher cover my afternoon Psychology class because I wanted to attend a memorial service for a friend of mine who had died the previous week. It was held in a large church about six miles from my home. I'd never been to the church before, nor had I seen or heard the pastor.

He was outstanding, and it was the most upbeat memorial service I've ever attended. He started by announcing to the more than 800 people in attendance that it would be a "celebration of life!" And it was. He built his brief service around three Scripture verses, and the key word in each of them was "joy" – as in the joy my friend Bob brought to his family, friends, and colleagues, and the joy he had found in life.

After only about 30 minutes, the pastor picked up a wireless hand-held microphone and walked down to the first pew. He said, "I kept my part of this celebration short so you could participate in it. Would anyone like to share a memory about Bob? If you do, please use the mike so everyone will hear you. At this point most of the 800-plus people froze. The number one fear of Americans is speaking in front of large groups of people. But the man standing next to me near the front of the church didn't have that fear, so he raised his hand. The pastor handed him the mike, and he paid a beautiful tribute to Bob.

This seemed to break the ice, and now hands were going up all over the church. The pastor was literally running up and down the center aisle and passing the mike all over the church because so many people had wonderful things to say about Bob. I couldn't help thinking about the day before in class, in which my students said it would be awkward and embarrassing to say something nice about another person, especially in front of 30 others. Here were people comfortably saying nice things about another person in front of more than 800 others! Then I thought about it a little longer and realized that an important element was missing – Bob. He wasn't there to hear all these wonderful tributes. Then I wondered how many of these people had said these things to him while he was still alive. My conclusion was that very few had, and sadly, maybe none of them. Bob was gone now, so it was safe to praise him.

The first time I told this story I wasn't sure how it would work. I spoke to the entire faculty of a large school district in Tulsa, Oklahoma. I thought it went well, and that I was able to make the point about showing our appreciation for people while they're still alive. A high school English teacher approached me immediately after I finished and encouraged me to tell the story everywhere I go. She also told me that she had an anonymous quotation that would fit well with the story, and asked me if I'd like to hear it. All teachers and speakers appreciate a good quotation, so I assured her that I'd love to hear it. Here's what she said:

> *A single rose*
> *is of greater value*
> *to the living*
> *than an entire wreath*
> *is to the dead.*

I realized immediately that it did, indeed, fit well with the story, and I've used it ever since. I also thought about it extensively on my way home that evening. While on the plane I wrote it out several ways and decided the version above is the best in written form. I also began tweaking it, and came up with the following, which I also use while telling the story:

> *A single kind word*
> *is of greater value*
> *to the living*
> *than hundreds of kind words*
> *at a memorial service.*

It had dawned on me during the memorial service that there was a powerful life lesson here about affirming words. Should we wait until after people die to say something nice about them? When I got back to my Psychology class the next day, I asked them if they remembered what we'd been talking about two days earlier. They did. One student said, "Oh, you mean that affirming language stuff?" I said, "Yes. Let me tell you a story." I explained in detail what had happened the day before at the memorial service. Then I asked them a question: "How many of those people said those things to Bob while he was still alive?" I guess they all agreed with me, because most of them were shaking their heads no.

At this point I threw out a rhetorical question. I didn't have the answer, and I didn't expect them to have the answer, either, but I thought it would get us moving towards one. I asked, "Do you think we can come up with some technique or strategy that makes it comfortable for us to say nice things to each other?" There was silence for a few moments as we all pondered the issue. Then a hand went up in the back of the room and Nancy announced excitedly, "Oh, Mr. Urban, I know how you can get us to say nice things about each other easily!" I was pleasantly surprised. Maybe Nancy knew something the rest of us didn't. I said, "OK, let's hear your plan."

"Simple, Mr. Urban. Just bring a casket into the class and put it up front. Open the top half, and we'll take turns sliding in. I'll go first." Then she held up a yellow hi-liter and said, "You be the pastor, Mr. Urban, and this can be your microphone. I'll be lying in there, and you ask, 'Would anyone like to say something about Nancy before we close the casket?' They'll be saying all these great things, and I'll be in there just digging it!"

Teachers laugh uproariously when I tell this story in person because I think they form a picture of this little activity going on in their own classrooms. I don't know if it's as funny in writing. But Nancy's point was well taken, and even the kids laughed.

But it presented me with a problem. I didn't know if Nancy was being serious, kidding, or both. But I *did* know that I didn't want a casket anywhere near my classroom. So I attempted to get out of it gracefully and ended up saying the dumbest thing I ever said in 35 years in the classroom. I said, "Oh, Nancy, that's a great idea. The only problem is that I don't know where we'd get a casket." It's at this point that teachers laugh the loudest because they all know how much teenagers love a challenge, and I'd just given them an intriguing one. As soon as the words slipped off my tongue I realized what I'd said. And I was now living proof of something I'd taught them earlier – you can't take your words back. But it gets worse (funnier).

Sitting in one of the front seats, less than two feet away from me, was Walt. I'll give you just one guess as to what his dad did for a living. You guessed it – he was the local mortician. I glanced at him and thought, "Oh, no. How bad can this get?" Walt was a real laid-back kid. He looked up at me, smiled, slowly raised his hand, and said, "That won't be a problem, Mr. Urban. Which model do you want?" At that point we got a little sidetracked because the kids wanted to know about the various models. They were astounded to learn that some of higher-end caskets cost more than their car did. This was an opening for me. I said, "Let's see if we can get back on track. And while we're doing it, do you think we can affirm each other without using any props?"

So we started on a new venture – building up instead of tearing down. Was it awkward and embarrassing for them? Yes, it was. At first. But like any new skill we learn, the more we practice it, the easier and more natural it becomes. Some kids became better at it than others, but they all got it, and they all agreed that it was a much better way to go. That was in the spring of 1972, my sixth year of teaching, and I'll always remember the students in that class. They were the pioneers who proved that we can teach kids (even teenagers) how powerful positive words can be. Let me repeat something I said earlier: This is one of the most valuable concepts I ever taught during my entire career. I continued to teach it for the next 29 years, until I left the classroom in 2001. I was always proud of my students because they nourished the classroom instead of poisoning it.

The other ways in which we nourished the atmosphere will be discussed at length in the next chapter.

A great suggestion from a student

*Listen to your students. They often see things
that teachers don't see.*
– Professor Robert Crowley

I learned early in my career to listen to my students. I frequently asked them to tell me what was working, what wasn't working, and how we could make a class better. They have a different perspective than we do, and they can help us become better teachers if we ask them to. In the early 1970s, when I was in the early stages of my crusade to teach kids that positive words can have powerful results, a student made an invaluable suggestion. His name was Chris, and he was one of those rare teenagers who came to class every time for the right reason. He came to learn.

On the day I introduced the concept of building up instead of tearing down, he remained after class for a few minutes. He said, "Mr. Urban, I not only understand *what* you're trying to teach us, but I understand *why* you're teaching it. We all put each other down way too much, and someone should have taught us otherwise a long time ago. I really support what you're doing. The only problem is that you're asking us to do something we rarely do, and to make it even more difficult, you're asking us to do it in front of 30 other people, some of whom we hardly know." He added, "We need some one-on-one practice." I immediately recognized the value of his suggestion and told him that I'd work on something to give them that opportunity. At first, I thought I'd pair them up in class, but it seemed a little too contrived. So I came up with a homework assignment instead. It turned out to be one of the best I ever assigned.

Due on: _____ Name_____ Per. ____

Affirmation Assignment
(verbal)

"Words go into the body. They can cause us to be well and hopeful and happy and high-energy and wondrous and funny and cheerful." – Maya Angelou

Assignment: Use your words to make someone else feel one of the things Maya Angelou mentions above. Give three people a verbal affirmation – one that is personal, not physical (hair, clothes, looks, etc.). Make someone feel good.

Person: _____ Relationship:_____
What you said: _____
_____
_____
Response: _____
_____

Person: _____ Relationship:_____
What you said: _____
_____
_____
Response: _____
_____

Person: _____ Relationship:_____
What you said: _____
_____
_____
Response: _____
_____

10 point assignment: 3 for each affirmation and response; 1 more if I can read it

The kids had a lot of questions when I first gave the assignment. Here are a few of them:

- "How do I pick the person?"
- "What should I say?"
- "Should I write down the response then or wait until later?"
- "Should I tell the person that it's an assignment?"

Here were my answers:

- "Any three people you appreciate." In fact, I asked them if there were three people who worked at the school whom they appreciated. They all said yes. I asked them, "When was the last time you told one of those people?" Answer: "Never." My comment: "Maybe now's a good time."

- "How about opening with one of these two questions?"
  1) Do you know what I like the most about you? (Tim Hansel's wonderful question), or 2) Would you like to know why I appreciate you?

- "I would wait until later."

- "Only if the person asks. If the person does ask, tell the truth, but also remind her that you could have picked anyone, and still chose her simply because you appreciate her so much."

The kids came back to class the next day feeling very happy for some good reasons. One – They found it to be an enjoyable assignment. It led to much more conversation beyond the initial compliment. Two – They made someone else feel appreciated. Three – It felt good to do that. Four – It was easy. They also were eager to share their assignments with their classmates, especially the responses they'd received. A number of them said, "She actually cried." Some people go so long between receiving expressions of appreciation, when they do get one, it bowls them over emotionally.

One of my students told her mother that she loved her and appreciated everything she did every day for the family, even though she rarely tells her. Her mother broke down in tears because she felt so *un*appreciated and had been starving for that kind of acknowledgment. The girl and her mother ended up having a long conversation that was beneficial to both of them, as it cleared the air about how people often take those closest to them for granted.

The funniest one I ever read was from a boy named Tyrone, a student in my Psychology class in the 1999-2000 school year. This is what he wrote:

Person: "Serena"

What you said: "I didn't say anything. My lips did all the work."

Response: "Hers were doing the same."

Even though he gave me a good laugh (without trying), I couldn't give him his three points for that one because it wasn't verbal. I circled "Use your words ..." on his assignment and gave it back to him with this little note: "Thanks for the good laugh, but this isn't verbal – no points for being a lover." His response, in a good natured way, was, "That's cold, Mr. Urban. See on the assignment where it says, 'Make someone feel good.' Well, I made Serena feel goooooood!" Another good laugh – but still no points. I promised him I'd give him a chance to get them back on a future assignment because he'd supplied me with some great material for my presentations and eventually a book. He felt good about that.

We discovered that some people become very suspicious when you give them a genuine compliment. Some people rarely get praised, so when they do, they conclude that they're being manipulated. One of my students says, "I want to tell you why I appreciate you so much," and the adult responds with, "What do *you* want?" What was supposed to be a win-win assignment just became lose-lose because the student gets flustered, says, "Forget it, then," and walks away. I told my students that if this happened, they should be mindful of their body language and tone of voice, look the person in the eye, smile, and say pleasantly, "I just wanted to tell you why I appreciate you. I don't want anything else." Then the ball is handed back to the adult, they end up talking, and they almost always work their way back to a win-win situation.

My favorite letter

I've always believed that the greatest reward teaching offers is the opportunity to influence a young person in a positive and lasting way. Sometimes we do it and never even know we had such an impact. Sometimes we do it and learn about it years later. It's wonderful when a student, and possibly a parent, thank us at the end of the year for being such a good teacher. But what's far more wonderful is receiving a letter from a former student several years later, telling you that you had a positive and permanent impact on his life. I've been blessed by many of these types of letters over the years, but the best one ever came near the end of my career in the classroom. It came from Bill, one of the greatest students I ever had the privilege of teaching. He'd been a teacher's dream – and then some. He was bright, imaginative, funny, positive, energetic, hard-working, polite, and genuinely curious about life. Like I say – a teacher's dream. I remember writing to his parents, and somewhere in the letter saying, "He seems too good to be true." And he really did.

Bill had graduated from high school in 1997, went to Yale, and was graduating from there in 2001, the same year I was finally graduating (retiring) from high school. Here's what he wrote:

May 16, 2001

Dear Mr. Urban,

It seems like I just left Woodside High School a short time ago, and now I'm graduating from college in a few more weeks. I've been thinking about you a lot this past month, and thought I better get it down on paper. I remember you always told us that if we had something good to say about anyone, to say it.

I remember vividly how you covered the "TOXIC" and "NOURISHING" words thing early in the school year. I agreed with your ideas, but I was a little skeptical about the affirming language stuff at the beginning. To be honest, I thought it was a little corny. But I'm glad I gave it a try because, as you know, I became a total convert. It's a valuable social skill I took to Yale and one I'll use for the rest of my life. Thank you for teaching it to us. I've never taken words for granted since I was in your class.

The lessons on affirming language helped me in four ways: 1) I became aware of the awesome power our words can have, so I developed the habit of choosing them more carefully. 2) I learned to look for the good, especially in other people, and I now find opportunities everywhere to comment on it. I always have something good to say. 3) I found out that once I got started, it became natural and easy to use more life-affirming language. 4) Every time I make someone else feel good, I can't help feeling better myself.

Thank you for making a difference. I hope to see you when I'm home in a few weeks.

Sincerely,

Bill

The No Poison Pledge

At the end of the first two days of school I asked my students if I'd succeeded in helping them become more aware of the power of words. They assured me that I had. I asked them if they'd be willing to sign a voluntary pledge to help keep the toxins out and put nutrients into the classroom atmosphere. While there were always a few who didn't sign, almost all of them did. It was a simple two-part promise:

I'm aware that many words act like toxins. They poison the atmosphere. I'll do my best to avoid using any of the Dirty Thirty categories while in this class.

I'm aware that other words act like nutrients. They nourish the atmosphere. I'll do my best to use words from the Thoughtful Thirty categories while in this class.

Date: _____   Signature: _____

I don't really know if the pledge itself made that much of a difference, but my students told me it did. They said when they signed something it was more of a commitment; they were more likely to live up to their promise. And they almost always *did* live up to their promise. They did an excellent job of nourishing the atmosphere rather than poisoning it.

Do not let any unwholesome talk come out of your mouths, but only what is helpful for building others up according to their needs, that it may benefit those who listen.

Ephesians 4: 29

Good teachers start every class with something positive

The best use anyone can make of any day is to enjoy it – and then spread that joy to others. Let us celebrate today!

– John Kremer

Bad news to good news

In the early years of my teaching career I developed a one-page current events homework assignment for all my U.S. History and American Government students. In my history classes, I wanted to use current events to tie the past with the present. In my government classes, I wanted to use newspapers to show how all levels of government operate. Once my students got the hang of it, they could scan a newspaper, select five relevant items, write a brief summary of each, and earn 10 grade points. They could complete the assignment in 10-15 minutes. They also could earn two extra-credit points by taping a political cartoon to the back of the main assignment and briefly explain it.

I worked very hard on developing this assignment, and to be honest, I was pleased with the final product. Because a good teacher also is a good salesperson, I did my best to convince my students that there were several benefits to doing it regularly. I told them they had opportunities to: work on their time management skills, practice self-discipline, develop a positive daily habit, become better informed, carry on intelligent conversations with other well-informed people, impress both their peers and adults, complete the assignment in a short period of time, earn valuable grade points, and pad their point total by doing some extra-credit work. In short, I was trying to sell them on the idea that it was an awesome assignment!

Being the young and naïve teacher that I was, I assumed my students would all respond favorably to the opportunity to achieve so many things in a mere 10-15 minutes. I didn't exactly expect them to give me a standing ovation while chanting, "Yay, homework!" – but I *did* think they'd see all the benefits of such a simple assignment. Wrong! I was still learning that students have a Pavlovian response to words they consider to be truly offensive. One is "homework." The other is "current events." Put the two together and you have a nasty little combination. What did they do? They complained, whined, moaned, and groaned. What did I do? I smiled, held up my faux can of poison spray, pointed out that we'd had a little accidental seepage, and reminded them that we needed to nourish the atmosphere, not spray toxins in it. Keep in mind that the "TOXIC – NOURISHING" concept was still new to them.

I promised them that after doing it a few times and becoming more familiar with newspapers, they'd truly appreciate the assignment. I said, "This might be one of the quickest, easiest, and most beneficial homework assignments in the history of education! It's so good you should be *begging* me for it!" Truthfully, most of my students did come to see the merits of current events homework, and they did it well. Of course, there were always a few who didn't. Homework and current events were either against their religion, as in "Thou shalt not do homework," or against their philosophy of life, as in "I don't do homework." Unfortunately for them, I had an opposing philosophy that said, "Thou shalt not pass students who don't do homework."

It usually took about two weeks for all of the students to become comfortable with the assignment. Not only did they become better informed and improve their grades, but their new awareness of what was going on in the world (besides popular culture) led to some great class discussions. Then, out of the blue one day, a student named Jason said, "You know, Mr. Urban, for being such a positive guy, you sure do give a negative homework assignment." I was mildly shocked, and thought maybe he was kidding. I asked, "*Me*, negative? How could such a win-win assignment be negative?" His response was simple, and it made perfect sense. He said, "Reading the newspaper can be a real downer. Do you realize that most of the news is *bad* news?" It was a point well taken. I've always wondered why the news media favors bad news more than good news. I've been told that it sells better.

I told my students that Jason's point was well taken, and I agreed that there was more bad news than good, at least in the newspapers. I said, "Well, maybe after reading and writing about all the bad things going on in the world, we should balance it up by sharing some of the good things going on, especially in *our* lives. How about if we reserve a few minutes at the beginning of every class – right after you turn in all the bad news – to celebrate the good news? Does anyone have some good news today?" This occurred in the early 1970s, and I still remember it as if it was yesterday. Here's the good news I heard the first time we did this:

- "My Dad has been looking for a job for almost a year. He finally found one even better than his last job, and got hired yesterday."

- "I got my driver's license three days ago."

- "I made the baseball team."

- "My sister got engaged last weekend. Everyone in the family loves her fiancée."

- "I finally understand algebra. With the help of a tutor I raised my grade from an F to a B."

- "My Mom and Dad have been separated and in counseling for about four months. My Dad is moving back in next week, and I'm sooooo happy!"

- "I got tickets for the Giants–Dodgers game this Saturday."

One of the unexpected joys that came from this simple little activity was the way the kids turned it into a celebration. When the first girl told about her dad being hired for his new job, applause broke out spontaneously. So each news item that followed also received applause. I couldn't help thinking, "What a simple, yet great, way to start class every day!" And the more the kids got into it, the more they shared – big things, little things, in-between things, family news, school news, sports, music, achievements, new purchases, etc. – nothing was off limits if it was something positive and sincere. A lot of kids used to ask me at the door, "Can I go first today?" They were genuinely excited to share their good news.

In the second year I did this, I received a note at the end of the year from Laura, who was the valedictorian of her class. In it, she told me that she often worked so hard at being the perfect student, she too often got bogged down with "all the serious stuff." As a result, she often forgot to notice that there were good things going on all around her every day. She wrote, "Thank you for reminding us that there's actually more good going on than there is bad. It just doesn't get as much publicity. I always looked forward to coming to your class because I knew I'd have two positive experiences right at the beginning – your warm greeting at the door and the time for sharing good news. Those two simple things always lifted my spirits, whether I was in a good mood or a bad one."

A second option – Who or what are you thankful for?

Being thankful is a habit – the best one you'll ever have.
Title of Chapter 7, Life's Greatest Lessons

As much as I enjoyed hearing the kids share their good news and sharing mine with them, I later came to the conclusion that we needed to tweak the activity a little. The news and the applause were always great, but not enough kids were involved. The quiet and shy students never volunteered anything. I didn't want to make them feel uncomfortable by forcing them into something, but I wanted to figure out a way to get them involved. If I called on them and asked if they had any good news, they would simply say, "No." I needed a better question to draw them in.

If you've read any of my previous books you already know that I'm big on thankfulness. I consider it to be both the healthiest attitude and the healthiest habit you can possibly have. I've always thought of being thankful as "perpetual good news" because most of us have so many good people and things in our lives that we should never take for granted. So when I called on a few of the quiet kids in class and they told me they didn't have any good news, I asked a second question. "Well, then do you have any special people or special possessions in your life that you're thankful for?" They *all* had both, and it was generally easy and non-threatening for them to answer my question. Here are the most frequent answers I received:

People	Possessions
Mother	Home
Father	Computer
Brother/sister	Phone
Best friend	Car

People	Possessions
Grandparent	Television
Aunt/uncle	Clothing
Coach	iPod or MP3
Pastor	Money
Teacher	Food

If you're wondering which answer I received the most, it was "My mom" by far. I always followed immediately with another question: "Why are you so thankful for your mom?" It's an easy question to answer, even for the shyest of kids. And so were the other questions, whether they were about a person or an object. It's not difficult for any of us to explain why we appreciate our favorite people or things. And because this question was asked and answered a few times every day, we heard expressions of thankfulness every day. This had two major results: First, it had a build-up effect. The more times we heard students talk about who and what they were thankful for, the more we were reminded to be appreciative of all that we have. Secondly, it helped bring to light something I told my students at the beginning of every year. I simply said, "There's far more in life to be thankful for than there is to complain about." They didn't get it at first because we live in a culture of complaint. But they *did* get it shortly after we started sharing this "perpetual good news" every day.

About two months after I added this second option, one of my brightest students, Taylor, stayed after class one day to discuss it with me. He said, "You know, there really *is* a lot more to be thankful for than there is to complain about. I can see now why you have us do this. Even on days I don't say anything about whom or what I'm thankful for, someone else always says it for me. Sharing good news and expressing our thanks seems like such simple things to do, yet they have a profound effect when they're done regularly. It kind of changes a person's outlook." I couldn't have said it better myself.

About five years after I implemented the good news and expressions of thankfulness into the daily routine, I ran into one of my former students who had recently graduated from college. She asked me, "Do you still start class the same way?" I said, "Absolutely! I can't imagine *not* starting class that way." She said, "You know, Mr. Urban, I don't know where you came up with that idea, but it sure is powerful. I was in your Government class and I've forgotten who the Speaker of the House is, but I've never forgotten to share my good news, ask others to do the same, and be thankful for all that I have." I hugged her and said, "Thank you. I promise to keep doing it for as long as I'm a teacher."

A third option – Who has a kind word?

*Kind words are short and easy to speak, but
their echoes are truly endless.*
– Mother Teresa

In the previous chapter I explained how I taught my students to use affirming language with each other rather than put-down language. But I didn't want it to be just an intellectual concept, something that remained in their heads but never transformed into behavior. It was important to give them an opportunity to actually practice affirming each other on a regular basis. The time at the beginning of each class in which we shared good news and expressed our thankfulness seemed to be the natural place for it. So we started with good news, later added expressions of thankfulness, and then added a third option – saying something positive about a classmate.

These were the guidelines we established for affirming one another:

- The positive comment must be sincere.

- Physical characteristics and possessions were out of bounds – looks, hair, clothing, body, physical prowess, jewelry, car, cell phone, iPod, etc.

- The compliment could be spoken directly to the recipient or it could be in the form of an announcement. Example: "I want to tell everyone why I appreciate Jim so much. He's the best listener I know. He always makes you feel like what you have to say is important."

Keep in mind that using this kind of language is something new for kids. It takes some time before they become comfortable with it. Every class is different because the chemistry and the relationships within each are different, but if the teacher is patient, acts as a good coach, and is encouraging, they'll learn to affirm one another.

A fourth option – Make us laugh

Of all the gifts bestowed by nature on human beings,
hearty laughter must be close to the top.
– Norman Cousins

At the beginning of my second year of teaching, I had what I thought were two brilliant ideas. As it turned out, one was and one wasn't. I wrote about the first one in Chapter 4 – greeting my students at the door every day, every period. As simple as it was, it had a major effect on helping me make that all-important daily connection with my students. My second brilliant idea was to tell a joke at the beginning of each class. I figured each of my students would get a nice warm greeting and a good laugh, putting them in just the right frame of mind before we started in on the academic rigors of the day.

I didn't need any material to greet them at the door, but telling a joke every day obviously did require some material – more than I could have ever imagined. I had about 15 good, clean jokes at the time. I figured I'd use them in the first three weeks of school, then buy some joke books and find one a day after I ran out. It sounded simple. But the truth is that I created a monster for myself. To begin with, my 15 jokes had all gone over very well with adults, but not as well with kids. Have you ever noticed how different their senses of humor are than ours? Some of my best jokes turned out to be what the kids called "groaners." To make matters worse, I discovered that good jokes (especially ones that kids will laugh at) are hard to find, even in a book with more than 300 jokes in it. I found myself often spending more time looking for a joke than I did on a lesson plan. This was definitely *not* a brilliant idea. In fact, it was a horrible idea because of the pressure I placed on myself.

Somehow I managed to struggle through that first year of joke-telling. I came up with more than 180 jokes, and probably about 60 of them actually mustered up some laughs. I didn't know if I had it in me to come up with 120 more that would work with kids. Fortunately, my students did appreciate what I was trying to do. They would good naturedly ask, "Do you have another corny/lame/unfunny (take your pick) joke for us today?" One girl even told me, "You know, Mr. Urban, you're funny even when your jokes are bad. At least you're trying to make us laugh." That was a real confidence booster.

What I learned from this well-intentioned but painful experience was to never place that type of pressure on myself again. I became convinced that not even the most accomplished and hilarious professional comedians had 180 jokes that kids would laugh at. In my third year I told a joke (one that had a successful track record) about once a week. But I still believed that starting every class with a laugh was a good idea, even if it didn't seem humanly possible. I continued to think about it for the next couple of years. There just *had* to be a way. The idea would return some day under a new format.

It was a few years later when we started sharing good news at the beginning of each class. Then we added the expressions of thankfulness. Then we added the kind and affirming words. Then another light went on inside my head! How about if I add "make us laugh" as a fourth choice and let the kids come up with the humor instead of me? Again, it seemed brilliant, but it didn't work. Keep in mind that all of this was voluntary, and they had four options each day. My students did an outstanding job of sharing good news, expressing thankfulness, and affirming each other. But they rarely chose the "make us laugh" option. The reason was simple. My rule was that if they told a joke it couldn't be mean-spirited or dirty. Sadly, those were the only kinds of jokes most kids knew, so they avoided this new choice. Another brilliant idea bit the dust.

But I was determined, and at some point in my third year of teaching I finally discovered a formula for laughs that worked. I assigned two students daily to "Laughter Detail." That meant that each day, right after we shared good news, expressed thanks, and affirmed one another, two kids would make us laugh before we got to work. If I had 30 students, it meant that a student had "Laughter Detail" only one time every three weeks. They were OK with that, and they accepted the challenge. I chose two students instead of one each day in case one was absent or one "forgot" the assignment. It worked better than I thought it would, and the kids came up with some very funny stories (often about their families) and a surprising number of good, clean jokes.

I want to conclude this chapter with one of my favorite stories about the "Laughter Detail" assignment. It took place at the beginning of a school year in the 1990s. I had a girl named Alma in my first period Psychology class. I knew her well because she'd been in my U.S. History class the previous year. Alma was a beautiful, sweet, intelligent, and conscientious student. She was also one of the shyest students I'd ever taught. It was her bad luck to have her name drawn for the first "Laughter Detail" assignment of the year. And she did exactly what I predicted she would do. She stayed after class so she could privately ask me to release her from this horrendous duty.

I told her I would never want to make a student feel uncomfortable in my class and that I wouldn't force her to do the assignment. But I also reminded her that she had signed up voluntarily for my Psychology class, and that I'd made it very clear that it was a course about personal growth and development. I told her that this would be a golden opportunity to take a little step outside her comfort zone and have some fun at the same time. I told her I wouldn't make her do it, nor would I penalize her in any way if she chose not to. But I also got her to promise me that she would use her imagination and energy to come up with something that would make her classmates and me laugh. So we reached an agreement – she would genuinely try to come up with something funny, and I would let her off the hook if she failed.

The next day she let me know at the door that she was going to make us laugh. I was overjoyed, and told her I was proud of her for accepting the challenge. This was a big step for a girl as shy as Alma. I silently prayed that she really did have something funny. I didn't want to see her bomb or make her classmates groan. When we finished sharing good news, expressions of thanks and affirmations, I announced that it was time for a few laughs. I called on the other kid, Joey, first. He told a hilarious story about a family car trip.

Then I called on Alma, and she floored me. The students weren't required to get out of their desks to do this, but Alma got up and walked confidently to the front of the room. I couldn't believe what I was seeing. She looked at everyone, smiled, and then reached into the pocket of her jacket. She pulled out one of those king-sized Snickers candy bars. She held it up above her head and said, "Whoever laughs the loudest gets this." There was a moment of silence, then an eruption of laughter. There were three boys in the class that really wanted that candy bar. They proceeded to make complete fools out of themselves in their efforts to win the prize, and the laughter grew louder by the minute. It became infectious, and we were all roaring. Apparently it was louder than I thought, because the teacher across the hall came over and shut my door. I apologized to her later. And what was Alma doing this entire time? Beaming!

I told her later how proud I was of her, and she admitted that it was an important step outside of her comfort zone. I asked her where she got the idea. Her answer was, "I just used my imagination." I have several other stories about funny things kids came up with, but they'd fill too many pages. I'm confident that your students will be just as funny as mine were. Laughter is good for the soul.

> *A man needs a little madness or he never does*
> *cut the rope and be free.*
> — *Zorba the Greek*

Good teachers, along with their students, have a mission

Mission
A specific task that a person or group of persons
is sent to perform; an allotted or self-imposed
duty or task; calling.
– Merriam-Webster's Collegiate Dictionary

A great life lesson from a weekend retreat

Until the early 1980s, I paid scant attention to mission statements. I was aware that businesses, churches, and schools often posted them in conspicuous places, but I rarely took them seriously. They often appeared to be lofty and idealistic statements about the values and purpose of the organization. But I couldn't help wondering who wrote them and how many people in the organization were even aware of them, let alone bought into them. I probably felt that way because my own school had a mission statement that seemed like a bad joke. To begin with, it was poorly written. A vague school mission statement with a grammatical error in it doesn't exactly fuel the passion and renew the purpose of the educators who work there. One of our English teachers pointed out the error to the principal, and was told, "Oh, it's no big deal. It's just a statement that the district requires us to write." So much for having a mission.

My limited perception and cynical attitude about mission statements changed dramatically in one weekend. A number of my friends were going to a men's retreat in the Santa Cruz mountains, and they invited me along. Everything about the weekend seemed promising. The speaker was well-known and respected, and he had a provocative title: "What's Your Purpose?" The retreat was in a beautiful setting only an hour from home, with comfortable accommodations and excellent food. I'd be surrounded by friends, make new friends, and maybe even learn something of value. As positive as my expectations were, I had no idea that this would be a life-changing experience – personally, professionally, and spiritually.

The leader of the retreat started with this question: "Why are you here?" The first person he called on answered, "Because my wife thought I should attend." The second person replied, "Retreats are always restful and re-energizing." And a third man responded with, "A lot of my friends were coming." The retreat leader then clarified his initial question. He said, "I don't want to know why you're here this weekend. I want to know why you're here on earth. What's your purpose in life?" That was a bit different. The room became silent as we grappled with the enormity of his question.

Then he asked another question: "How many of you have a written personal mission statement that you look at and think about every day?" There were about 150 men there, and not one hand went up. Most of us had never heard of a personal mission statement. He said, "That's OK. It just means that I have my work cut out for me this weekend." He said he had two goals for the retreat. The first one was to help us answer the question in the title of the retreat: "What's Your Purpose?" The second goal was to help us put our answer into writing in the form of a personal mission statement. He achieved both goals.

Although I wasn't thinking about school in the early stages of the retreat, the speaker said something that made me do just that. He said, "All good organizations with a purpose have a well-crafted mission statement. It gives the people within them both focus and clarity, and it inspires them to fulfill that purpose." Then he added, "Don't you think the same principle applies to individuals? Shouldn't every good person with a purpose also have a well-crafted mission statement?" He completely sold me on the idea, and I did go away from the retreat with a concise personal mission statement that I've looked at and dwelled upon every morning for more than 25 years. It does, indeed, add focus, clarity, and a sense of purpose to one's life.

While we concentrated on personal mission statements throughout the weekend, I couldn't help thinking from time to time about what the speaker said regarding "all good organizations with a purpose." I thought about it even more on my way home Sunday afternoon. I had a completely different sense of what a mission statement was, and I began to see some wonderful opportunities to apply it at school. I was always looking for "life lessons" I could bring to the classroom, and I was convinced that the retreat leader had provided me with a valuable one. It turned out to be more valuable than I could have ever imagined.

It dawned on me that I was the leader of five "organizations with a purpose" – my five classes. This realization led to some questions:

- Could I help my students see and clarify that purpose?

- Did they know what a mission statement was?

- If they didn't, could I teach them?

- Should my students and I write a mission statement together?

- Or should the teacher and the students have separate missions?

- Would any of this make a difference?

I've always had the philosophy of "nothing ventured, nothing gained," so I went for it. I decided that their mission was different than mine, and that I'd write one as the teacher and they'd write one as the students. The way the kids responded to the idea of writing their own mission statement and the difference it made astonished even a positive guy like me.

The teacher's mission

*Every teacher in the world, whether working with a
pre-kindergarten child or a Ph.D. candidate, has
the same mission – to bring out the best in the student.*

– Professor Erwin G. Hall

I left the weekend retreat with a written personal mission statement, but it wasn't something I could use at school. It wasn't specifically tied to my responsibilities as an educator, and it contained references to God and my spiritual beliefs. So I decided to write a separate mission statement, one that applied solely to my role as a teacher.

Back in Chapter 6, I shared with you a profound quotation by child psychologist Haim Ginott on the difference a teacher can make. Remember that I covered it with clear plastic, taped it to my desk, and read it the first thing every morning upon entering my classroom. It served as a wonderful reminder about the awesome responsibilities I had every Monday through Friday. But it was too long and too general to serve as a mission statement. I decided to leave it where it was as an expression of my philosophy of education, and to place right next to it a more concise teacher mission statement that I'd be able to share with my students.

I went to work on it as soon as I got home on Sunday afternoon from the retreat. After about six or seven hours, six or seven thousand thoughts, and several pieces of paper, this is what evolved:

My mission as a teacher – A promise to my students

- My ultimate responsibility as a teacher is to bring out the best in my students, to help them perform at their highest levels in both academics and character.

- I'll treat you with the utmost of respect – the same way I expect you to treat me and your classmates.

- I'll do everything in my power to create the best possible classroom atmosphere, one in which I can teach and you can learn.

- I'll come to each class prepared with a meaningful lesson plan.

- I'll be consistent in maintaining high academic standards while supporting my very strong belief that there's no substitute for hard work.

- Whenever possible, I'll try to connect school to the larger world outside. I'll teach "life lessons" along with the academic lessons in each course.

- I'll make myself available to help you in both academics and personal matters.

- I will <u>always</u> give you my best.

When I was finished, I hand-printed it (there were no computers in those days) as neatly as possible with a black felt tip pen. The next morning I placed it on my desk at school, right next to the Ginott quotation, covered it with clear plastic and taped it down. It was worth all the time I spent on it. While my personal mission statement has changed a few times over the years, this teacher mission statement never did. It stayed exactly as it's written above during the remaining 20 years of my teaching career. Reading it and the Ginott quotation every morning was a positive and powerful way to begin my teaching day.

The students' mission

The first time I experimented with this new concept, I began by asking the students in all of my classes if they knew what a mission statement was. Out of more than 160 students, there were about four or five who did. Obviously, I needed to provide a definition and a few examples. I explained that another term for "mission statement" was a "statement of purpose," and that businesses, service organizations, charitable foundations, places of worship, schools, universities, and even individuals used them to stay focused on their goals. I showed them the mission statements of our school, the University of San Francisco, the Girl Scouts, the Rotary, a local church, Apple Computer, and UPS. All my students had a pretty good idea of what a mission statement was by the time we were finished.

I shared with them that I had both a "philosophy of education" (the long quotation by Haim Ginott) and a "teacher mission statement" taped to my desk. I read them out loud to each class and invited them to look at them any time they wanted. I also told them to bring it to my attention if they ever thought I was acting in a way that was inconsistent with my philosophy or my mission. Yes, it did happen a few times. Posting your own specific mission statement for the students to see keeps you focused, diligent, and accountable.

I asked the students if they thought I should write their mission statement for them (often referred to as the top-down process) or if they should write their own. I asked because I already knew what the answer would be. One girl said it succinctly: "It wouldn't really be *our* mission statement if *you* wrote it, would it?" I answered "No. I think you'll honor it more if you own it."

I divided them into six groups of five or six students and gave them these instructions:

> 1 – The mission statement could not be longer than two sentences. Mine was longer, but I wanted theirs to be shorter so they would get right to the point.

> 2 – The mission statement could be about one of two topics – either the environment we were going to create in the class or the process of learning itself.

It turned out to be a very engaging activity for two reasons. First, they had learned an important new concept – a mission statement. Second, they had the immediate opportunity to develop their own and begin putting it into practice. Each succeeding year I looked forward to this activity because the students always took it seriously and enjoyed the process. Over the years they came up with some wonderful mission statements. Here are a few of the more memorable ones:

Atmosphere/Environment

> **"THIS IS A GOLDEN RULE CLASSROOM. WE PRACTICE WHAT WE PREACH."**

> **"THIS IS A NO PUT-DOWN ZONE. WE LOOK FOR THE GOOD INSTEAD."**

> **"THIS IS A PLACE TO BE NOURISHED. NO TOXINS ALLOWED."**

Learning/Knowledge

> **"WE COME THIRSTING FOR KNOWLEDGE."**

> **"LEARNING IS NOT AN OBLIGATION; IT'S AN OPPORTUNITY."**

> **"CAME TO LEARN!"**

Frequently asked questions

"If you had six different groups working on mission statements, how did you settle on the one for the entire class?"

Simple – I let the students choose. Because they were all brief, I wrote each group's mission statement on the chalkboard. Everyone could see what the other groups came up with. I told them they could pick a statement as it was written or combine parts of different statements, as long as it ended up no longer than two sentences.

"Do you end up with five different mission statements (one for each class) or one for all your classes?"

I left that up to my students. The day after each class selected their mission statement, I put all five on the board. They had two choices: stay with the one they chose yesterday, or adopt one from another class they liked better. Some years I had the same mission statement for all five classes. Other years I had five, four, three, or two mission statements, depending on how the kids voted. I always felt that the more we had, the better it was. The students in each class saw their own mission statement as well as the mission statements of the other classes.

"Do you show your students the mission statements that were written in previous years to help them get started?"

No. I was afraid it would influence them too much. I wanted each class's mission statement to be their own, and with five to six kids brainstorming on the idea, they always came up with something good.

"Did you reserve the right to exercise veto power?"

Yes, and I told them so at the beginning. It didn't happen very often, but on occasion a group didn't mesh, or a group wasted too much time playing around (it's one of the hazards that accompany group work). If they didn't come up with a satisfactory mission statement in class, each student was assigned the task of writing one on his or her own for homework that night. They learned early on that it was better to get it done in class with the help of four or five classmates.

The mission must be visible

If at the beginning of every school year I taught my students what a mission statement was, provided them with examples, and had them write one together, it would always be a valuable lesson. They'd learn a new term that would reappear often in their lifetimes, and they'd have hands-on experience in writing one. But if I said, "OK, that's your mission," then erased it from the board and never came back to it again, it would fade from their minds quickly. If this lesson is to be truly meaningful it requires another step.

Step two is just as important as learning what a mission statement is and being able to write one. It absolutely *must* be posted in the classroom. Not on a 3 X 5 card taped to my desk or on an 8 1/2 X 11 sheet of paper thumb-tacked to a side wall. I'm talking something big. Here are the minimum requirements:

- Written on a large poster board at least 4 feet wide and 3 feet high.

- Written in a bright color on a white background.

- Written in the largest letters possible.

- Posted in the front of the room where every student sees it every day.

Each teacher would do this a little differently due to his or her conditions. In my case, I asked the kids how many were currently taking an art course. There were always seven or eight who were. I suggested they see their teacher (there was only one art teacher), and that he would provide them with a large white poster board. They would put the mission statement on it in large brightly colored letters, add a few decorative symbols, earn art credit, and bring it back to my class. It would be placed right above the chalkboard in the center of the room. They couldn't avoid seeing it if they tried. Any time they looked at the front of the room, there it was, staring them in the faces and reminding them of their mission.

This was a remarkably simple lesson and activity that took up about 40 minutes, sometimes more. But like the time we spent on manners and the Golden Rule on the first day of school, it was well worth it. It paid dividends for the rest of the year. I was always pretty focused in the classroom, but writing a separate teacher mission statement gave me even more clarity. Reading it and the Haim Ginott statement the first thing each morning always seemed to reaffirm and strengthen my purpose. It worked the same for my students. Class is a lot more meaningful when they come in with mission.

> *All good organizations with a purpose have a well-crafted mission statement. It gives the people within them both focus and clarity, and it inspires them to fulfill that purpose.*
>
> *– Kent Shields*

> *There are no right or wrong ways to express your mission. The important thing is to identify a mission statement that is uniquely yours.*
>
> *– Hyrum W. Smith*

Good teachers use the power of visible reminders

Visible reminders help students stay focused.

– Professor Vanessa Soucy

Repetitio est mater studiorum.
(Repetition is the mother of learning.)

– Latin proverb

Stories, activities, and a reminder for each

In Chapter 7, I explained how an empty can of Lysol became a symbolic can of poison spray. It was always prominently displayed on my desk. I wanted my students to see it every day so they'd be reminded to not poison the atmosphere of the room. None of them wanted to be the cause of me picking up the can and saying, "Oh, we've had a little accident. Someone let a little poison out of the can." I also diagrammed the six signs with the universal red circle and slash that were around the clock on the wall to my right. They reminded my students that there would be no put-downs, complaining, whining, moaning/groaning, swearing, or gossip in my room. In Chapter 5, I explained the Golden Rule poster in the back of the room. And in the previous chapter I explained how the mission statement was turned into a large, visible reminder.

This chapter is about the signs that were in the front of the room along with the mission statement. They were all on colorful sheets of paper, had large bold letters on them, and were laminated in clear plastic. If you walked into my room on the first day of school you wouldn't see any of them. If you walked into my classroom after the first two weeks of school you would see all of them. That's because putting them all up before the first day of school wouldn't do any good. They'd add some color to the room, but they wouldn't add any meaning. I learned to put them up a few at time over the first two weeks, right after I told a story or we did an activity. This way, each time a student looked at one of the signs he or she would be reminded of the lessons that had come with them.

The first sign of the year was a single word – **CHOICES**. It was accompanied by four additional signs (each with a story) that answer this question: What are the four most important choices you'll make in your lifetime? Although these were the first five signs to go up, I'm not going to explain them until Chapter 14 (no fair peeking ahead). That chapter is devoted to our responsibility as teachers to help our students understand that they make important choices every day, and to help them discover the most important ones they'll ever make.

The second set of signs had to do with manners and the Golden Rule. Since we had devoted much of the first day of school to them, I wanted to have some reminders in the front of the room. Here are the three signs the students saw:

THE
GOLDEN
RULE
RULES

This sign was the result of our discussion after I taught my students this universal principle of good human relations. One girl in the class said, "If we'd all practice the Golden Rule, we wouldn't need any other rules." Another student added, "Yeah, the Golden Rule rules." Keep in mind that besides this sign in the front of the room, we had the poster in the back with 15 versions of the Golden Rule on it.

**NO ONE
EVER
WENT WRONG
BY BEING
POLITE**

This sign went up after asking everyone a simple question. First, I reminded my students that I'd studied a lot of history in college and had been teaching the subject in both high school and in a university for many years. Then I asked, "In the history of the human race, do you think anyone ever went wrong by being polite?" Quite a discussion ensued. It started with the "cavemen," then progressed to the Egyptians, to Europe, to the prim and proper British royalty, and finally to the United States. None of us figured out exactly how good manners originated, but we all agreed that mutual respect was always win-win, and that no one had ever gone wrong by being polite. Up went the sign.

**NO
DISCOUNTS**

**EVERYONE
COUNTS**

This sign also went up after a question and a discussion. The question was, "Do you know what a discount is?" Of course the first answer was always, "That's when prices are marked down, when there's going to be a sale." I said that was one kind of discount, but I wanted to talk about another kind, one that dealt with human relations and often caused hurt feelings. This is my definition of a discount: When you treat someone as if he or she doesn't count; when you act like the person isn't there; when you ignore him or her. I asked my students if this had ever happened to them. All of them said yes.

Then I asked another question: "Which is worse, a put-down or a discount?" There wasn't unanimity among their answers. Some said they'd rather be ignored than be viciously put down. Others pointed out that when someone puts you down, at least your presence is being acknowledged. When people completely ignore you, it's as if you don't even exist, and nothing is more painful. Personally, I think a discount is worse, and I shared that feeling with my students. In my career I saw a lot of kids get ignored by both classmates and teachers, and I could see the pain, alienation, and loneliness it caused. We did all agree that discounts were harmful to the classroom atmosphere, and that not paying attention and not listening to others were the most common forms. Since we had agreed to a No Put-Downs policy, we also agreed to a No Discounts policy. Up went the sign.

I explained in Chapter 9 that we started every class with something positive. The students had four options: share good news, say something or someone you're thankful for and why, say something kind about a classmate, or make the class laugh. We had a sign that went along with this wonderful daily up-lifter. It's the one above, and if I could only have one sign in my classroom, this would be it. I always wanted to remind my students that there's much more in life to celebrate than there is to complain and whine about. So I started every class by pointing to the sign and asking, "What are we celebrating today? Who has good news? Who's thankful today? Who has some kind words? Who's going to make us laugh?" I've been out of the classroom for a few years now, but it always brings back good memories when I think about getting a warm greeting at the door and then having a mini-celebration of life before we went to work.

I was always a firm believer in teaching life lessons along with academic lessons. Mainly because I felt we never did a very good job of teaching our students how life works in the real world or helping them figure out what the essential ingredients of a successful life are. One of the life lessons I wanted to pass on to all of my students had to do with effort, determination, diligence, and good old-fashioned hard work. When I was growing up, the messages I received about being successful in life were pretty straightforward. I got them at home and at school and at church. I also got them from a variety of employers and coaches. Even television and the movies reinforced the simple idea that if you wanted to be good at anything, you'd have to work hard. It was a healthy message because that's the way life does indeed work. That's why I wrote a chapter in my first book, *Life's Greatest Lessons,* entitled "There's no substitute for hard work."

Unfortunately, that's not the message many of our young people are getting today. In fact, they're often bombarded with messages that claim the opposite. Some of them are:

- The good things in life come *quickly* and *easily.*

- You *deserve* a good life.

- You can have it *all,* and you can have it all *now.*

- You don't have to make any sacrifices to get what you want.

The longer I taught, the more I was disturbed by the "instant gratification" philosophy of life so many of my students seemed to buy into. I felt both a professional and a moral obligation to help them understand that the images they see on TV, in magazines, in videos, on the Internet, and in movies don't really reflect life as it is in the real world. As I did so often in teaching them life lessons, I started with a question. I asked them, "Why would you ever want to give less than your very best?" The initial responses were always additional questions, as in "Where?" and "When?" My answer to both was, "Everywhere and all the time." Most of them thought that was impossible, so we always got into a provocative discussion.

Here are some of the questions, along with my answers, that I got most frequently from my students:

- How do you give your best when you're just socializing with your friends? Give them the best you have. Have fun with them, laugh with them, play with them, let them know how much you enjoy being with them.

- How do you give your best when you don't feel well? You give the best you can under those circumstances.

- Do you think there's anyone who gives his or her best *all* the time? Yes, I think millions of people do.

- How often do you give *your* best? All of the time – teaching, meeting home responsibilities, being with my family, writing, reading, working out, playing sports, spending time with friends.

The concept of *always* giving your best was new to them, so my answers prompted even more discussion. They found it hard to believe that there were millions of people, including me, who always gave their best. Many still believed that it was impossible. Most of them equated giving your best with struggle, superhuman effort, stress, exhaustion, and being too serious all the time. This led to the heart of the discussion because it's this way of thinking that prevents people from giving their best. I explained that life is far more rewarding when we do the best we can no matter what we're doing, where we are, or whom we're with. To make my point more clear, I said we could give our best even when we're having fun or resting. It's not a matter of stress or being too serious. It's a matter of being in the moment and making the most out of it. An example I always used was teaching. It requires very hard work, but it can be fun at the same time. In fact, the harder I worked at it, the more fun I had, and the more rewarding it was.

I asked them if they wanted me to give my best every time they came to my class. The answer was always yes, along with this little addition: "You're supposed to give your best because you're getting paid." This always brought a smile to my face, as I informed them that I was paid to teach, not to give my best. There's a big difference. I chose to give my best because it made my teaching so much more enjoyable and fulfilling. They were starting to get it.

My students concluded that there were primarily two reasons that people often chose to not give their best: laziness and self-centeredness. It was a point well made, and I agreed. I concluded by pointing out that we reap what we sow. "What does that mean?" immediately followed. I explained that we get out of life what we put into it. Then I asked them the same question I started the lesson with: "Why would you ever want to give less than your very best?" And up went the sign. I was always confident that I planted some important seeds during this lesson. Hundreds of times students told me, "I can't get that question out of my mind." I loved it! It was music to my ears.

OPPORTUNITY

Above is one of my two favorite words in the English language. As with many of the others, the lesson began with a question: "Is going to school an obligation." Almost everyone answers yes. Then I ask, "Why is it an obligation?" Answers: "Because we *have* to go." "It's the law." "You can't get a good job without an education." "My parents make me go." I asked them if they'd go to school if it were optional. About 95 percent said yes. I said, "Well, if you'd go to school even if it was your choice, then why not look at it as something more positive than as an obligation?" Their response was, "What do you mean?" I asked, "Why not look upon coming to school as an opportunity?" And their response was again, "What do you mean?"

It was at this point that I shared some vivid stories. Travel has been a high priority with me for many years, so I've seen much of the world. Sadly, I've seen a lot of poverty and thousands of young people who were out working in the fields instead of learning in classrooms. They'll never have the opportunity to go to a school. They'll never have the opportunity to improve the quality of their lives through education. Why do so many people in other countries want to come to the United States? Because we have more freedom and opportunity than any other country. How do you increase that opportunity? By getting an education. Up went the sign.

POSSIBILITIES

This is my other favorite word, and with it came one of my favorite activities. I handed out a small piece of paper to each student. Then I asked them this question: "Would you agree with me that in the history of the human race there have been thousands of great achievements that have made the quality of life better for us?" Yes was the only answer I ever received. I told them I was going to ask them another question, and that I wanted everyone to write down their answer before we had a discussion. I told them we weren't going to argue about what was the greatest achievement, but we were going to talk about some of them. I said, "Please write down one that stands out to you as among the greatest." It took less than two minutes for everyone to answer.

I then asked each student in the class to share his or her answer. Here are some of the most frequently repeated answers I received: putting a man on the moon, cars, telephones, cell phones, iPods, CDs, computers, the Internet, TV, airplanes, electric lights, great works of art, famous buildings and structures, the collected works of Shakespeare, the civil rights work of Martin Luther King, Jr., Abraham Lincoln's handling of slavery and the Civil War, music, literature, education, sports, democracy, and capitalism. There were many others as well, but they came up much less frequently.

My next question was, "Do you realize that every one of these great achievements had exactly the same starting place?" This always resulted in some puzzled looks, but someone always got it. He or she would ask, "Mr. Urban, do you mean that they all started as an idea?" That's *exactly* what I meant. They all started in someone's imagination, which comes from the word image, or picture. Someone got an idea first, then formed a picture, then went to work on something that had never been done before. My most important question was, "Were these people thinking in terms of obstacles and reasons why it couldn't be done, or were they thinking in terms of possibilities?" I added, "Nothing ever gets done, big or small, unless someone believes it's possible. They got it. Up went the sign.

This was one of my favorite signs because one of my students thought I needed it. He printed it out from his computer, found out where I had my signs copied on colored paper and laminated, went there, and had it made. One day during our "good news" time he announced to the class that he had a new sign for the room. He said, "Mr. Urban says this so often, it might as well be posted on the wall." He showed it to the class and they all laughed. It was true. I did say it several times a week.

I always wanted to challenge my students to see the opportunities, to see the possibilities, to give their best. And I frequently reminded them that they would never make any progress, never fully develop, unless they were willing to take some steps outside their comfort zones. In other words, "There's no parking in the comfort zone." I loved the new sign.

These are only some of my signs. I wanted to provide some examples of how I used them. You may want to use some of the same ones, you may not want to use some of them, and you may want to develop a few or many of your own. I promise you, if they're accompanied by a good story or activity, they'll serve as powerful reminders for your students.

> *The world does not require so much to be informed*
> *as to be reminded.*
> — *Hannah More*

Good teachers help their students both own and honor the rules

Students should have a voice in making the rules that apply to them; once rules are established, however, students are expected to follow them.

– William Glasser, M.D.
Schools Without Failure

"People behave as they're expected to behave"

The first time I heard the above statement was when I was a 19-year-old sophomore at the University of San Francisco. I was in my first-ever Sociology class, not really sure I even knew what the subject was about. I signed up for the class for the same reasons most college students sign up for elective courses: other students told me that the subject was interesting and the professor was great. Both were true. The professor, Dr. Ralph Lane, was a college student's dream: knowledgeable, passionate, interesting, caring, and funny. He was one of my all-time favorite teachers.

On the first day of class he told us that students who majored in other subjects often signed up for Sociology without really knowing what it was. I was one of them. He said, "Let's start with Principle No. 1: People behave as they're expected to behave." He went on to explain the relationship among sociology, psychology, and cultural anthropology. They each involved the study of human behavior, but from different perspectives. The focus in sociology was on how people are influenced by others and how they behaved in group settings. He also explained that people function more successfully when they know what's expected of them – whether at school, at work, in a place of worship, in a social setting, or participating in athletics. In a matter of a few minutes we all had a pretty good grasp on the subject of sociology. And I never forgot that people behave as they're expected to behave, especially during my many years as a classroom teacher.

I learned early in my career that handing out classroom rules wasn't the best way to begin a new school year, so I postponed it until the second week. I figured that if I could sell the Golden Rule and good manners as win-win propositions on the first day of school, and if my students bought into them, we could start the process of establishing expectations without imposing rules. Teaching lessons about toxic and nourishing words in the first week also helped establish expectations, especially when my students signed the pledge regarding the type of language we would and would not use in the classroom. But rules still are necessary. The key is to establish them in the right way, and in the right spirit.

Anarchy or order?

I've mentioned a few times previously that I often started a lesson with a not-so-common word or a challenging question. In this case it was the word *anarchy.* I asked my students if they knew what it meant. As you might suspect, some did and some didn't. I read the following from the dictionary: "Anarchy – a situation in which there is a total lack of organization or control; the absence of any form of government, rules, or order." Then I asked the following questions and offered the answers that I felt applied to them.

Q: What would happen if our country had no rules? A: It would be a disaster.

Q: What would happen if our school had no rules?   A: It would be chaos.

Q: What would happen if this class had no rules?   A: No one would learn.

Q: Which would you rather have, anarchy or order? A: Order.

Kids of all ages and their teachers understand that there's a need for rules and there's a need for someone to be in charge. In fact, one of the things students will be the most vocal about in their criticism of particular teachers is that they have no control over the class. Kids will act up and break the rules at times, but they still want their teachers to have a firm grip on things. They want the teacher to be in charge, and if you're a teacher who isn't, the kids will run all over you – then complain that you don't have control over your students.

Another vocabulary lesson

Back in Chapter 7, I explained how I put the words "TOXIC" and "NOURISHING" on the chalkboard to start my lesson on the power of language. I did something similar to start my lesson on the need for rules, leadership, and order. I put two more words on the board in large letters:

STRICT   MEAN

Then I asked them two questions: First, "Do you know the meaning of these two words?" They all answered yes. Second, "Do the two words have the same meaning?" Most of them said yes, a few said no. It was time for the dictionary again. Here's what I read to them:

"Strict – closely observing rules, principles, or practices"

"Mean – cruel or bad-tempered; unkind or malicious"

Then I repeated my second question: "Do the two words have the same meaning?" Now they were beginning to see the difference, and understand why I wrote them on the board. Just as I wanted to be proactive earlier regarding manners, I also wanted to be proactive about establishing the rules of the class. Too many students see "strict" and "mean" as the same thing. If they ask you for permission to do something and you tell them no, they'll often respond by saying, "You're mean." I always responded to that accusation by saying (with a big smile, of course), "No, I'm not mean, but I *am* strict. There's a big difference between the two words." After this had happened a few times, I came to the conclusion that it would be more effective to define both terms early in the year.

After putting the words on the board and reading their definitions, I told my students, "I don't have a mean bone in my body, and no matter what the circumstances are, I will *never* be mean to you. But you also need to know that I *am* strict. Once we establish the rules, they'll be closely observed. If you tell me I'm mean, I'll say, 'No, I'm strict.' If you tell me I'm strict, I'll say, 'Thank you,' and consider it a compliment." This little vocabulary lesson was always effective in laying the groundwork for writing the rules. One of the most important points to be made here is that a teacher or parent can be strict and caring at the same time. It's often called "tough love," and it's exactly what kids need.

An invaluable lesson from Dr. William Glasser

I had two incredible learning experiences during my second year of teaching. The first one occurred at school in the Fall semester. I was taught that, "What you accept, you teach." That was discussed in Chapter 5. The other great lesson occurred during the Spring semester, about 500 miles away from school. It was my good fortune to be selected as one of two Social Studies teachers at my school to attend a statewide conference in San Diego, California.

While I was excited about going to the beautiful city of San Diego, I was even more excited about being taught by Dr. William Glasser. I had read three of his books, the most recent one being *Schools Without Failure.* It's one of the best books I've ever read regarding schools and teaching, so I was thrilled to have the opportunity to learn in person from the author. He did not disappoint. In fact, he had an enormously positive impact on the remaining 33 years of my teaching career. I, in turn, have shared what he taught me with thousands of other teachers since beginning my speaking career in 1995. A great teacher's influence lasts forever, and Dr. Glasser was that great teacher.

Someone once said that all great ideas are simple. Dr. Glasser presented us with an idea that was so simple – and so obvious and logical – that none of us had ever even thought about it. He was talking about the need for reasonable rules, both on campus and in the classroom, and the need to consistently enforce them. He said the problem with most rules was that they were handed down from above as if they were edicts coming from God. The people most affected by these rules, the students, had no opportunity to participate in the drafting of them.

He reminded us that participatory democracy is at the heart of everything we do in this country. He referred back to how the earliest settlers to come here governed themselves, to the steps leading up to the American Revolution, to the war itself, and then to the democratic process that resulted in the writing of our great Constitution. As a U.S. History teacher, I could fully appreciate what he was saying.

Glasser suggested that we needed to invoke those same democratic principles when writing the rules in our schools, no matter what the ages of the students. Then he said something I never forgot:

"If you want the kids to honor the rules, give them some ownership of the rules."

He suggested that one of the most effective ways to help students become responsible was to give them a voice in the rules and procedures affecting them on a daily basis. Then he asked this simple, yet brilliant, question: "Why don't you let your students help you write the rules?" He said he guaranteed that they would behave more maturely and more responsibly if we did. And he was exactly right. I couldn't wait to get back to my school and start implementing his ideas.

The only problem was that it was late in the Spring semester, and the more I thought about it, the more it made sense to wait until the beginning of the next school year. I had plenty of time to think about it, read more of Glasser's works on education, and play around with ideas on how to best get my students involved in writing the rules in my classes.

The result was a remarkably simple handout that had remarkably powerful results.

Names _____

IF WE MADE THE RULES

Students would not be allowed to...

1) _____

2) _____

3) _____

4) _____

5) _____

Students would be encouraged to...

1) _____

2) _____

3) _____

4) _____

5) _____

Procedures for giving students ownership of the rules

I'm sure there are many ways to do this. All teachers have different personalities, teaching styles, subjects to teach, communities to teach in, and students of different ages, so I don't think there's any *one* way to write the rules together. I'm just sharing the procedure I developed, so feel free to do the same thing, or any variation of it that works best for you.

Step 1 – Ask the students if they'd like to write the rules

I guarantee this question will get their attention. Since we'd already established the need to have rules, my students were more than willing to take on this responsibility.

Step 2 – Divide the class into small groups of 5-6 students

I gave each group one copy of the "If we made the rules" sheet, asked them to select a recorder, and gave them 15 minutes to collectively write down the five most important "do's" and five most important "don'ts" for the school year. This was one of the two most engaging group exercises I ever did. The other one involved the writing of the class mission statement, which was explained in Chapter 10.

Step 3 – Have each group report out on their rules

When they were finished, I asked group No. 1 to share their five top "don'ts." I wrote each of them on the board so everyone could see them. Then group No. 2 added the ones they'd written that weren't covered by the first group, and so on, until every group had been heard from. Not surprising was the fact that many of the groups came up with the same ideas. "Students should not be allowed to be disrespectful" was by far the most repeated rule. We used the same procedure regarding the "do's."

Step 4 – Write up a master list of the year's "do's" and "don'ts" from the groups

I wanted to give you an example of actual student rules, so here are the ones my students wrote in September of my last year (2000-2001) in the classroom. Most of them are self-explanatory, some of them are explained on the following page.

Class Rules – Do's and Don'ts in Mr. Urban's classes
(Written by the students and the teacher*)

You are allowed and encouraged to do the following in this class:

Honor the Golden Rule
Be respectful of teacher & classmates
Come to class "thirsting for knowledge"
Take good notes
Do your homework consistently
Participate in discussions
Have a positive attitude
Have an "Oh, boy!" attitude
See learning as an OPPORTUNITY
Listen to the teacher and classmates
Come to class prepared – binder, pen, etc.
Help each other learn
Bring good food on your birthday
Accept responsibility for yourself
Honor the rules we've written
Be in class on time
Have good attendance
Say "please" and "thank you"
Say positive things about your classmates
Share good news/celebrate the good
Express your thankfulness
Make people laugh without being dirty
Express your opinion
Be curious/ask questions
Be open to new ideas
Make others feel welcome
Do extra credit on homework assignments
Practice good manners
Act and be treated like young adults
Keep the classroom clean
Always give your best
Make suggestions
Ask if you need help
Maintain an organized binder
Learn something new every day
Cheer when you get handouts
Let Mr. Urban know if you're having problems*

You are not allowed to do the following in this class:

Discount/ignore other students
Discount/ignore the teacher
Leave your desk without permission
Interrupt when someone is speaking
Annoy others
Talk serious smack to others
Swear/use bad language
Put others down
Stay in your little clique all the time
Make sexist comments
Put make-up on in class
Have a bad/negative attitude
Litter/leave a mess behind
Have side conversations (no discounts)
Be rude/impolite
Block the aisle with your backpack
Put your gum under the desk
Throw things across the room
Invade other students' privacy
Come to class late – it's rude
Act like you're a bad dude (tough guy)
Write on desks, walls, posters
Make fun of/laugh at others
Dominate discussions
Act like a know-it-all
Speak without raising your hand first
Complain/whine (it poisons the atmosphere)
Run with scissors
Eat or drink in class
Cheat/lie/steal
Make irritating noises (gum popping, etc)
Give up on yourself
Gossip/spread rumors
Say "I need ..."
Make racist comments
Sit and do nothing (stay on task)*
Sleep or put your head down on the desk*

Explanations of the Do's and Don'ts page

The asterisk – There's one "do" and two "don'ts" that have asterisks after them. This means that I wrote the rule because I insist upon it, and the students failed to include it. I always remind them that I have the ultimate responsibility for the class, and that if a rule is important to me, I'll add it to their list and be diligent in enforcing it.

"Let Mr. Urban know if you're having problems*" – This is my way of telling them at the beginning of the year that I'll help them in any way I can, whether it's an academic or personal problem. They're also assured that I'll respect their privacy.

"Sit and do nothing (stay on task)" – Because students are often allowed to sit and do nothing in other classes, their initial expectation is that it's OK in my class, too. It isn't. And I strictly enforce it. They would occasionally ask me early in the year when I was going to give them a "free day." My answer was always, "There's no such thing, at least in my class." I told them I was paid to teach, and it's their responsibility to learn. That doesn't happen by doing nothing or having "free days." If I was teaching and a student wasn't staying on task, I would call on him or her and ask, "What are you doing?" The answer was always the same. It's the same one-word answer kids always give to that question, no matter what they're doing – "Nothing." I say politely, "I'm sorry, but you're not allowed to do that in my classroom, so let's get back on task."

"Sleep or put your head down on the desk" – This is another thing that goes on way too much in classes across the country. It did not go on in my class. I gave my students fair warning that these were two of my strictest rules, and that I would enforce them. Did heads ever go down? Yes, because many teachers hand out rules and then don't enforce them. So they tested me early on. I warned them about what I would do – walk over to their desk and knock on it loudly. It was very effective in keeping heads up. I told my students if they're sick, they go to the nurse. If they're not sick, they hold their heads up. I heard all the excuses at the beginning of each year: "I'm tired; I didn't get enough sleep last night; I was working late; I was doing homework." This was my response (with a smile and a pleasant tone): "Guess what? I'm tired also. I didn't get enough sleep, either. I had to work late, too, because teachers have lots of homework every night. But look at how young you are and you're sitting down. Now look at how much older I am than you and I'm standing. If I can stand, you can hold your head up."

A further note on the above two rules – Kids seem to think that they have a Constitutional right to sit and do nothing in class. I remind them that I have a bachelor's and a master's degree in history and have taught it for many years. I assure them that I've studied in depth the Declaration of Independence, the Constitution, the Bill of Rights, and all other documents pertaining to our freedoms as Americans. Then I tell them (with a big smile), "I promise you, you have no protected right to sit and do nothing or to put your head down on the desk. Case closed."

"Talk serious smack to others" – I didn't know what it meant either, so I made sure it wasn't something dirty they slipped in on me before I included it on the list. I found out that "smack" was the word being used that year for bragging. OK, no smack.

"Run with scissors" – This was a joke, but I left it in because it made me laugh. These rules were written by 12th graders. One group conjured up memories of their second-grade rules and thought it would be funny to slip this one in. It *was* funny. It's the only rule that wasn't serious.

"Bring good food on your birthday" – We had a school rule that said no food in the classroom. Unfortunately, many teachers didn't enforce it, so I was the "bad guy" because I *did* enforce it. My students accepted my decision to honor the rule, but they good-naturedly told me we should have an exception on birthdays because that's the way you celebrate everything – with food. Here was the birthday exception to the no-food rule: If it was your birthday – they all want everyone else to know it – you came to class with a bowl or plate of small goodies. You stood at the door with me as I greeted students, and you gave them a tasty treat. They knew it was your birthday as soon as they saw you next to me, wished you a happy one, consumed the little morsel before entering the room, and we were all happy.

My favorite rules – These were my favorite rules on the "Don't" side: Discount others, Have side conversations (no discounts), Have a bad/negative attitude, Complain/whine (it poisons the atmosphere), Say "I need …" These were my favorite rules on the "Do" side: Follow the Golden Rule, Come to class "thirsting for knowledge," Have an "Oh, boy!" attitude, See learning as an OPPORTUNITY, Say "please" and "thank you," Be thankful, Have good manners, Always give your best.

All-time favorite – "Cheer when you get handouts."

These were my favorite student-written rules because it meant that my students were buying what I was selling in the first week of school. I put an enormous amount of passion and energy into creating the best possible environment I could. I did everything imaginable to sell them on the ideas of mutual respect, the value of learning, positive attitude, hard work, and nourishing words. The rules written by my students were clear indications that they bought into these concepts because they were free to write any rules they wanted.

What about consequences? This is a frequent question. My guess is that the issue of consequences for violating the rules could be handled in several different ways. My approach was simple: If someone violated a rule, I would call "time-out" by making the "T" sign with my hands while looking at the student culprit. The "T" sign meant that whatever we were doing came to a halt. The student causing the time-out had two responsibilities. The first was to stop what he/she was doing (usually a side conversation). The second was to apologize to the class. Then we moved on without wasting any time. No need to yell, no need to write the kid up, no need to send him/her to the office. How about the more serious violations? They were rare, so I handled them on a case-to-case basis.

The bottom line – When teachers and students work together in writing rules based on mutual respect, they create a wonderful environment for both teaching and learning.

Mutual respect includes mutual responsibility.

– H. Stephen Glenn, Ph.D.

Good teachers set high standards and have high expectations

Educators everywhere share a goal of creating a learning environment which fosters, demands, and celebrates high standards.

– Ron Berger
Teacher and author

Strict vs. permissive

Dr. Stanley Coopersmith (1926-1977) was a great psychology professor at the University of California, Davis. His area of expertise was children's growth and development, and much of his research was done with parents, teachers, and children of a variety of ages. I had read a couple of his books early in my teaching career, and was delighted to learn in 1971 that he was speaking in Palo Alto, a short distance from my home. I attended his lecture, which was entitled "Bringing Out the Best in Our Children," with high expectations. He didn't disappoint. His insights were invaluable to a young teacher who was still trying to get a grasp on adolescent behavior.

He started by talking about two types of parents. The first are those who make the rules clear for their children and are consistent in putting them into effect. They're often referred to as strict parents. The second are those who have few rules and allow their children far more freedom. They're often referred to as permissive parents. Dr. Coopersmith said that research shows that in most cases children of strict parents function better and have higher self-esteem than those of permissive parents. The reason is that when parents set guidelines for their children and are consistent in upholding them, they send a strong message. That message is, "We care about you and don't want you to do things that are harmful." On the other hand, the message permissive parents often send is, "We don't have the time or the energy or the interest to set guidelines for you. You'll just have to learn things on your own."

Dr. Coopersmith added that most people, whether children, teenagers, or adults, operate more effectively when they have clearly defined boundaries. Generally, people feel more secure when they know what they *can* do, what they *can't* do, and what they *need to* do. These guidelines are even more effective when they're explained fully and accompanied with good reasons for each. It also helps when people know what the consequences are when they operate within the guidelines and when they don't. "As I said," he repeated, "people behave as they're expected to behave." Echoes of Dr. Lane, my college sociology professor mentioned in the previous chapter.

It all made perfect sense, and it was an effective introduction to the study of child psychology. What I didn't know at the time was how valuable this information would become for use in my classroom. My logical mind told me that the principle applied at school as much as it did at home. Students behave as they're expected to behave, especially if those expectations are made clear to them. If the expectations are high for both academic achievement and behavior, and the students are assured that they'll be strongly supported, they'll perform at a high level. So set your standards high – and expect the best.

Teachers who establish high expectations of all students –
and give them the support they need to achieve these
expectations – have high rates of success in both academics
and behavior. Grades and test scores go up, and problem
behaviors go down. The school, the teachers, the students,
and their parents all win.

– Professor Erwin G. Hall

Put your policies in writing

There are some important reasons why your standards/expectations/policies should be put in writing and provided to both your students and their parents.

Here they are:

1 – It sets a professional tone. It's a way of letting them know that you're serious about establishing and maintaining high standards.

2 – Putting your policies into writing makes them more specific and clearly understood. It greatly reduces the possibility of a student later claiming, "I thought you said ..."

3 – It's good insurance. The students who do the least amount of work and still expect to pass are the ones (along with their parents) most likely to cause problems at the end of the school year. It's nice to have your written policies to support your position.

I learned from a mentor early in my career to put all of my policies in writing. There were only a few policies at the beginning, and some of them were a bit vague. But the more I learned about teaching, the longer and more specific my policies became. Below are the policies I maintained and upheld during my last several years in the classroom.

Woodside High School   **Social Studies Department**

Mr. Urban's policies and expectations

Rationale – Many years in the classroom have taught me to make my expectations as clear as possible to both my students and their parents early in the school year. Please read over the policies below. Feel free to ask questions if any of them are not perfectly clear to you.

Foundation – It's important for you to know that I have high expectations of my students in two important areas: **1) Academics** – I'm old-fashioned. I'm not afraid to make my students **work** for their grades. The subject matter isn't hard to understand, but both work and self-discipline will be required to succeed in my class. **2) Behavior** – I expect my students to treat me and their classmates the same way I will treat them – with **respect**.

Grading scale – Students earn grades in my class according to the following percentages:

A – 90-100% of the total points possible during the semester
B – 80-89%   C – 70-79%   D – 60-69%   F – 0-59%

Example: If the semester ends with a total of 840 points possible and a student earns 744 points on tests and assignments, the grade will be a B+. The student earned 89 percent of the total points possible. A student earning 480 points would fail the course because the total represents only 57 percent of the points possible.

Grade record – Every student will be provided with a grade record and will be required to maintain it throughout the semester. This means they will always know what grade they are earning in the course. When a test or assignment is returned in class, students will be required to update their grade records. They are required to turn it in at the end of the semester, as it is one of the assignments of the course. If a parent asks a student, "What grade are you earning in Mr. Urban's class?" and receives the answer, "I don't know," it will not be the truth.

Class participation – Education is an active process, not a passive one. Students are expected to ask questions, answer questions, and take part in discussions. A student who sits passively and relies on the other students to make class interesting and lively is the equivalent of a parasite, defined in the dictionary as "somebody who lives off the generosity of others and does nothing in return." I will not give an A grade to a student who does not participate and contribute to the class even if he or she earns 100 percent of the points possible.

Homework – I am not a teacher who believes in piling on long homework assignments on a daily basis. Many of our students spend more than seven hours per day on campus, participate in sports, hold jobs, and have other obligations. I try to be realistic and acknowledge the demands placed on them. At the same time, I think a regular and brief (15-20 minutes) assignment is fair. It helps students develop self-discipline and some time-management skills while becoming better informed. In my U.S. History and Government classes, the homework will be in current events, and will be done daily. My Psychology students will have short papers to write on a weekly basis.

Make-up work – All students who are absent for a legitimate reason when I give a test or hand out an assignment will be given a reasonable amount of time to complete their work without penalty. I treat each case individually because the circumstances vary greatly.

Work submitted late – I'll be honest. I don't like late work when there's no valid excuse. My policy is a strict one. If the work comes in one day late, the student will receive 50 percent of the points he or she earned. Don't bother to turn it in late after that. It won't be accepted and a zero will be recorded in my grade book.

Second chances on tests – I've been teaching long enough to know that students regard tests in very different ways. Most take them seriously and try to do well. Some refuse to study and take their chances. For some, tests strike fear in their hearts. No matter how hard they study, they suffer from performance anxiety and freeze up. For them, and any other student who wants to take advantage of it, I have a second-chance policy. If you couldn't master the material on the first try, try again. You'll earn my respect for making a second effort, and you'll earn the grade points you need. One restriction: the highest score you can earn on a second chance test is 75 percent. That's a C, which is always better than an F.

Attendance – There's a good reason why we have school attendance laws. The most important one is that you're not learning if you're not in class. I realize both students and parents can play all kinds of games regarding "excused" absences. Please honor both the letter and the spirit of the law. I can teach you a lot more when you're in class. My experience has taught me that excessive absences always cause problems for both the student and the teacher.

Being on time – The reality is that we have a serious tardy problem at this school, so much so that it's become part of our culture. That doesn't make it OK to roll into class any time you want. Simply put, it's a matter of respect. I consider it rude and inconsiderate to be late for class, especially if it occurs on a regular basis. Please honor my request to be in class on time.

Extra credit – This is one of the most misunderstood and abused terms in the history of education. Let me be clear about what it means, and what it doesn't mean, in my classes. It means you do the regular assignment, and then you do *extra* work over and above it to earn extra grade points. *Extra credit* does not mean *instead of* work. Don't sit and do nothing for a semester, finally figure out that you're failing, then come and ask me if you can do "extra credit" work to make up for all the work you didn't do when it was assigned. You will receive a firm (and probably surprising) "NO."

Help is always available – Whatever the problem is – academic, family, personal, other – I will always be available to help my students. And the help will be immediate. All you have to do is ask. You'll receive as much help as you need even if it means evenings or weekends. Whatever the problem is will be kept strictly confidential. Please let me know if you need help in any way.

Classroom do's and don'ts – There are certain standards of behavior which I expect all of my students to meet. The single most important one will be The Golden Rule – treat others as you would like them to treat you. The specific do's and don'ts will be written in class by the students. Our goal is to create a classroom environment in which everyone feels comfortable.

Students live up or down to a teacher's expectations.
– Timothy Clemons

More about "extra credit"

As mentioned on my policies page, I believe "extra credit" is one of the most misunderstood and abused terms in all of education. It has been for as long as schools have been around. Who misunderstands and abuses it? Students, parents, and, sadly, teachers. In fact, teachers are the worst offenders. They're the cause of students and parents not being clear on the concept.

The way I explained "extra credit" to my students was to equate it with overtime pay. If the standard workday is eight hours and you work 10 hours, you get regular pay for doing the job you were expected to do, and you get extra pay for the extra two hours. But you can't get overtime pay unless you work the eight regular hours first. Nor can you ask your boss to do overtime to make up for work you were supposed to do, but didn't.

I've always believed in rewarding hard work, so I gave my students an opportunity to earn a few extra-credit points on every assignment. But they had to do the regular assignment before they could tack on any extra points. Let me give you a specific example: In my American Government and U.S. History classes, there was a brief (about 15-20 minutes) current events assignment every night. The students were to summarize, in their own words, five of the top news stories of the day (could not be about sports or entertainment). Each one was worth two points, for a total of 10. If they completed this assignment and wanted to earn two extra credit points, they could tape a political cartoon to the back of the sheet and write a brief explanation of it underneath. Thus, on a 10-point assignment they could actually earn 12 points. Extra points for extra work – just like overtime.

The problem is that too many teachers have been allowing students to do "instead of" work and calling it "extra credit." Example: a student goofs off for an entire semester, and is about to fail the course. With about three days left, he goes to the teacher and asks if he can do some "extra credit" work to bring his grade up to the passing level. The teacher, wanting to be popular, can't say no, and grants the student his wish. Here's the lesson the teacher taught: "I really didn't mean what I said about my grading policies at the beginning of the year. What I really meant is that you can be lazy, do almost nothing throughout the course, and I won't hold you accountable. I'll even reward you for it at the end."

One of my U.S. History students came to me at the end of a semester in which he earned 86 points out of a possible 950. He asked, "Can I do some extra credit to make up for the points I need?" Trying to hide my astonishment, I casually asked him what he thought he could do to make up for all that work that he *didn't* do. His answer was, "I could run a lot of laps." Working even harder at hiding my astonishment, I asked, "What do you mean?" He said, "I could run as many laps around the track as you want me to in order to bring my grade up." By this time I'm dumbfounded. I asked, "What does running laps around the track have to do with the work you missed in U.S. History?" He answered, "I don't know, but that's what my P.E. teacher allowed me to do to make up for all the days I cut his class." Somehow, I think he missed the point. And so did the other teacher.

I've also had students tell me they received "extra credit" for cleaning classrooms, washing teachers' cars, helping a teacher move, and baby sitting. I'm convinced that there are even more amazing stories out there about the wonders of extra credit. But I don't think I want to hear them.

The story of Jonathan

Before I leave the bizarre world of "extra credit," I want to share a story I've told many times in my workshops. It's about Jonathan, a senior in my American Government class in the spring of 2000. In the early days of the new semester, I went over my "Policies and Expectations" page with the students. They already knew they had to pass the class in order to graduate in June. When I got to the section on homework, Jonathan raised his hand and said rather proudly, "Yo, I don't do homework." Not knowing where this was leading, I said, "Well, the homework adds up to 50 points per week, and overall, more than half of your grade. If you don't do *any* of it you won't be able to earn enough points to pass the class."

To reinforce his earlier point, he said, even more proudly and defiantly, "Well, I still don't do homework." He seemed to feel a need to establish himself strongly so both his teacher and his classmates knew his position. Without wanting to have a confrontation with him, I asked a simple and innocent question: "Why would you not do at least some of the homework if you need it to pass the class and graduate in June?" At this point he became a little belligerent and boldly proclaimed something he had apparently been dying to say: "I don't do homework because it's against of my philosophy of life." A few kids giggled, I smiled, and Jonathan looked as proud as he could be. I said, "Well, it looks like we have conflicting philosophies, because I don't give passing grades to students who don't do the required work." Jonathan wanted to have the final word, so I allowed him to. He said, "I still don't do homework."

Jonathan didn't study for tests either, and he didn't keep the required grade record, so at the end of the quarter he had 62 points out of 450 possible. In other words, he had earned about 14 percent of the points. He received an F at the halfway mark, and his report card was mailed home. He didn't say anything to me about it, nor did he start doing his homework. And I heard nothing from either of his parents. About five weeks later he was in an even bigger hole, and I was required by district policy to send home, via registered mail, a notification that he was failing the course and in danger of not graduating. I received a notice that his father had signed for it. Again, Jonathan said nothing, still refused to do his homework, and there was no attempt on his parents' part to contact me.

When we were preparing for the final exam and there were only four days left in the semester, Jonathan stayed after class for a few minutes. I knew exactly what was coming. He told me he had "been doing some thinking" and realized that he couldn't earn enough points to pass the class even if he "aced" the final exam. I said, "Jonathan, that's what the quarter report card and the failure notification were all about. They were supposed to get you going – but they didn't. Now it looks like it's too late." "Are you trying to tell me that there's no way I can pass the class?" he asked. I said. "That's exactly what I've been telling you since that day early in the semester when you announced that you didn't do homework." And, surprise of surprises, he asked, "Well, can't I do some extra credit work so I can pass?"

I said, "Jonathan, let me read to you something I read to you and your classmates, and gave to you in writing, on one of the first days of the semester."

I picked up my "Policies and Expectations" page and read the following: "*Extra credit* does not mean *instead of* work. Don't sit and do nothing for a semester, finally figure out that you're failing, then come and ask me if you can do 'extra credit' work to make up for all the work you didn't do when it was assigned. You will receive a firm (and probably surprising) NO." Then I said, "Jonathan, that's my answer – a firm NO." He was in disbelief, and I knew what was coming next. He said, "But all of my other teachers are letting me do extra credit. If you don't let me do it I won't graduate." I wanted to say, "Well, duh," but restrained myself. I said, "Jonathan, you can't pass this semester. Summer school is a four-week session. I suggest you take Government there and do enough work to pass." Still in disbelief, he stormed out, but once again he needed to have the final word, and I again allowed him to. He warned me sternly, "This isn't over yet!"

I knew it wasn't over yet, and I knew what was coming next. Later that day I received a phone call from Jonathan's father. He started this way: "Jonathan tells me you won't let him do any extra credit, so now he can't pass your class." I said, "That's not exactly true. Jonathan could have done extra-credit work every day of the semester. He chose not to. He also chose not to do the regularly assigned homework. That, along with failing test scores, is the reason he's not passing." His response was, "Why won't you let him do extra credit now?" I reminded him that there was a real difference between "extra credit" and "instead of" work, and that I'd made that clear to the students and the parents at the beginning of the semester and had given everyone a copy of my policies in writing. He didn't want to discuss that issue. Instead, he said, "How come all the rest of his teachers are allowing him to do extra credit work?" I answered, "I can't speak for his other teachers. Maybe they have a different definition of 'extra credit' than I do. But I need to stand by my policies." As Jonathan had earlier, he warned me, "This isn't over yet!"

I knew it wasn't, and I knew what was coming next. He would call the principal. To give her a heads-up, I briefly explained the situation. I gave her Jonathan's point total (98 out of 920 possible for 11 percent) and a copy of my policies. She assured me she would support me. And she did when Jonathan's father called later that day. He was astounded and gave her yet another warning, "This isn't over yet!" It wasn't for sure, and I wasn't surprised at what happened next.

Jonathan's dad had two more weapons in his arsenal. The first was Grandma. He called me the next day to ask me if I knew Jonathan's grandmother was coming all the way from Iowa to be at Jonathan's graduation. I said no. He asked, "Do you realize what this is going to do to her?" He was now digging into his little bag of dirty tricks. This is what Nightmare Parents do, especially at this time of year. I asked him how long Jonathan's grandmother was going to stay. He asked, "What difference does it make?" I said, "Summer school starts next week. If she can stay for four weeks she can see Jonathan get his diploma." He then asked, "So you're still not going to pass him?" I told him no, I wasn't. So out came his biggest gun of all. I'd heard it before. He said, "Well, I guess I'll just have to get myself a good lawyer."

By this time I was becoming a little irritated, particularly because I felt he was trying to bully me. I always worked hard at being patient and calm in these types of situations because getting angry only adds fuel to the fire. But I'm also human, and Jonathan and his dad were getting on my nerves. I said, "Mr. Herndon, don't get just one lawyer. Get a whole firm of them. I'll be wherever I need to be with my policies in writing, my grade book, the quarter grade, and the failure notice you received a month ago." He hung up. Jonathan did not graduate with his classmates. I don't know whether he went to summer school or not. I don't know whether Grandma came or not. And I never heard a word from any lawyer.

Creating a culture of high expectations

On the same day that I discussed my policies and expectations with my students, I asked them if they had expectations of me. They assured me that they did. I suggested that before we have a general discussion about it, I'd like each of them to write down some of those expectations. These are the "Top Ten" expectations they came up with most frequently over the years.

    1 – Make the class interesting (not boring)

    2 – Have control of the class

3 – Be nice (not mean – don't yell at us)

4 – Be fair in the way you treat people (no favorites) and in grading

5 – Be reasonable on homework

6 – Return tests and papers within a week

7 – Explain things clearly (don't assume we already know everything)

8 – Have a sense of humor; make the class fun (not boring)

9 – Be understanding; try to remember what it's like to be a kid

10 – Give us help if we need it

I was always impressed with their list of expectations. I promised them that I would give the best I had every day in those areas. I also shared with them a well-known quotation from Abraham Lincoln: "You can please some of the people all of the time; you can please all of the people some of the time; but you can't please all of the people all of the time." I reminded them that on certain days, some students would find the subject matter interesting while others wouldn't. Some students would think I was reasonable on homework and some (like Jonathan) would think I was unreasonable. The main point was to assure them that I loved teaching, and had high expectations of both them and of myself.

I told them they could expect two other things from me that weren't even on their list. I promised them that I would, 1) come to class every day with a good attitude, and, 2) come to class every day fully prepared. I said, "I will give you the best I have every day. That's a promise." I also told them that I wanted to challenge them to give me their best every day. I wanted to plant a seed within the first few days of school. I said I'd be more specific about it in a few weeks, after I got to know all of them better. I explain this challenge in more detail in Chapter 14.

Starting the year by explaining my standards and expectations, going over my policies, and giving the students an opportunity to say what they expected of me always worked in setting the right tone – high standards and high expectations.

Set high standards, have high expectations, and watch your students perform at high levels.

– Dr. Robert Cazenave

Good teachers help their students discover the power of choice

The greatest power that a person possesses
is the power to choose.
                        – J. Martin Kohe

An essential life lesson we all need to teach

My first book, *Life's Greatest Lessons,* which had been self-published for several years, came out in a fourth edition in 2003 with Simon & Schuster as the publisher. One of the results of selling the book to a mainline publisher was a "media tour." I flew from city to city, got picked up in stretch limos, stayed in fancy hotels, was taken to expensive restaurants, and appeared on more TV shows than I can remember. For someone who'd been a public school teacher for 35 years, it all seemed like an otherworldly, out-of-body experience.

But it wasn't the limos, the hotels, or the restaurants that fascinated me the most. It was what the TV interviewers wanted to talk about. All of them had advance copies of the book, and they all had time to select the topics – the subtitle is "20 Things That Matter" – they wanted to discuss with me. Without exception, every one of them wanted to zero in on Chapter 4 – "We live by choice, not by chance." They all seemed fascinated by this topic. In fact, many of them acted as if I'd discovered one of the ancient and previously hidden secrets of life.

Nothing could be further from the truth. Choices have been around for as long as the human race has. Unfortunately, people of all ages pay scant attention to their ability and power to make the most important choices of their lives. Instead, they put themselves on the equivalent of autopilot and breeze through life in blissful unawareness. When people don't exercise their power to make these choices, they allow someone or something else to do it for them. It could be other people, it could be popular culture, or it could be the advertising industry.

The TV interviewers also were fascinated that I taught "life lessons" along with the regular curriculum. Several of them asked me a remarkably similar question: "If you could only teach two or three of these 'life lessons' to your students, what would they be?" I smiled and said, "That's easy. Here are my top three: The power of choice, the power of words, and the power of goal setting." Again, they were most interested in the topic of choice. Because these TV interviews were usually less than five minutes in length, I never had the opportunity to discuss the specifics of what I taught about choices or how I taught them. Fortunately, I *do* have more than five minutes to write this chapter, so I'll share with you one of the most important lessons I ever taught.

Life is an exercise in mindless conformity

I started the lesson by writing the words above on the board. I then gave all the students a half sheet of paper and asked them to write what they thought it meant. I told them that after everyone had written something down, we'd have a discussion about it. A few were puzzled at first. They needed some clarification on the word "conformity." I told them it was doing what everyone else was doing, and that explanation seemed to help. They also needed some assurance that there would be no right or wrong answers.

Those seven words I wrote on the board consistently produced some of the best class discussions of my career. At the heart of each one was an exploration of who and what has the most influence on our lives, including our decision-making. We all agreed that the social institutions that have the most powerful effect on us are parents, friends, school, faith, and popular culture – the media in general, and the advertising industry in particular. After a lengthy discussion of the influence of all of these, many of my students were willing to admit that they weren't nearly as independent in their thinking as they thought they were. They also agreed that if we let them, popular culture and the media could turn our lives into exercises in mindless conformity.

I've felt for many years that one of the most valuable things we can teach our students, from age 7 on, is about the greatest power they'll ever have – the power to choose. The end of our discussion seemed like the perfect time to start the lesson.

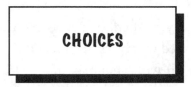

CHOICES

I mentioned in Chapter 11 that the first sign I put up was a single word – the one above. I showed it to my students and told them it would be on the wall the next day, with four additional signs underneath it. But before I put them up I wanted to do a little exercise with them. I handed out a half sheet of paper that looked like this:

Date: _____ Name: _____

LIFE'S MOST IMPORTANT CHOICES

What are the four most important choices (other than faith) that you'll make in your lifetime?

1 – _____

2 – _____

3 – _____

4 – _____

There were a couple of reasons why I left faith out of this exercise. The first is that I was teaching in a public school and felt it best to not bring religion in. Secondly, I wanted all the students, believers and non-believers alike, to be answering the question from the same perspective.

It takes students less than five minutes to list their four choices. They were not required to give reasons, and they were assured that there were no right or wrong answers. When everyone was finished, I asked if someone would volunteer to share his or her four answers. I always had several volunteers. I would select one and put his or her four answers on the board. Then I would ask the rest of the class how many of them had the same choices so we could put a total on each one. I followed that by asking for additional choices beyond those four. We usually ended up with about six more, along with a total for each. Everyone saw all the choices and knew how many students had selected each. Here were the four with the highest total each time I did this activity:

1 – Education

2 – Career

3 – Marriage

4 – Where to live

I told my students I agreed that these were among the most important choices we ever make. I had already made my choices in these four areas, and each of them has had a major and long-lasting influence on my life. I also pointed out that these were highly personal choices, and that we were unlikely to be heavily influenced by the media or other people in making them. They were feeling pretty proud of themselves that they were able to identify life's most important choices.

So they were a little surprised when I asked them, "Do you realize that there are four other choices that are a lot more important than the ones you selected?" I added, "In fact, you make each of them every day, and all four of them will influence your education, your career, your marriage, and probably where you choose to live. They're such important choices that they, more than anything else, will determine the quality of your lives – how happy, successful, and fulfilled you'll be, and how much peace of mind you'll have." I can assure you, they were all paying rapt attention. Several of them asked, "C'mon, Mr. Urban, what are they?"

I told them I had four more signs for them. They'd be on the wall the next day right under the sign that said **CHOICES**. It was important to point out that my four choices were one man's opinion, and that some great philosopher or billionaire businessperson or famous entertainer might disagree with me. I told them my four choices were based on what I had read in hundreds of books, what I had learned by going to school for more than 25 years, what other people had taught me, the insights I had gained from world travel, and most important, what I learned from many years of life experiences. The first sign I showed them was this one:

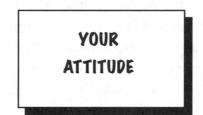

They looked surprised, and I knew exactly why. No one had ever told them before that attitude is a choice. I began with a question: "What determines your attitude at any given moment?" Here are the most frequent answers I received:

"It's determined by the mood I'm in."

"It depends on whom I'm with."

"What day of the week it is."

"Where I am."

"What I'm doing."

"The weather."

I said, "If your answers are all correct, then your attitude will always be determined by something outside yourself. You have no control over it. Your attitude is held captive by people, places, and conditions." Then I added emphatically, and with a big smile, "WRONG, WRONG, WRONG! I am now about to teach you the most valuable thing you'll ever learn from me.

Here it is: Aside from faith, attitude is the most important choice you'll ever make. You make this choice every minute of every day, and it will influence everything you do in life. Your attitude is the engine that runs everything. And it will ALWAYS be your choice, no matter what the circumstances are." The room became silent. It was the sound of thinking, and I loved it!

This was an entirely new concept to the kids, so they had to process it. And they had some legitimate questions. The most common one had to do with handling a tragedy. Here's a question I remember vividly: "So if your best friend gets killed in an accident, are you supposed to be happy about it?" I answered, "No, you're not supposed to be happy about it. You and all the other people associated with your best friend will go through a grieving process. You'll hurt over the loss, and you'll cry a lot. That's normal. But at some point you have to accept the fact that tragedy does happen, that bad things do happen to good people, and you need to move on. When we lose a dear friend or a family member, the best way we can honor that person is to keep the memory alive and dedicate a portion of our lives to him or her."

I remind my students that life doesn't always work as portrayed on TV and in the movies. And it doesn't work as portrayed in commercials, either. The good things in life don't come the "quick and easy" way, and you can't really "have it all, and have it now." We still have to make some sacrifices along the way, and we still have to work hard for the things that are important to us. Along with the joys and triumphs of life come the hard knocks, the disappointments, the failures. The issue isn't whether or not they should happen. The issue is what attitude we choose in dealing with them. Will we cave in and give up, or will we resolve to learn from them and become stronger?

> *Life is a series of problems. Do we want to*
> *moan about them or solve them?*
>
> *– M. Scott Peck*

At this point I had my students read Chapter 2 of *Life's Greatest Lessons*. The title is "Life is hard ... and not always fair," and it begins with this paragraph:

Life doesn't always work the way we'd like it to. If we had our way, it would be easier, consistently fair, and more fun. There'd be no pain and suffering, we wouldn't have to work, and we wouldn't have to die. We'd be happy all the time. Unfortunately, we don't get our way. We get reality instead. But reality is a great teacher. It helps us learn, although often slowly and painfully, some of life's most valuable lessons. One of them is this: The world will not devote itself to making us happy.

My students read the chapter, and then we discussed it at length. I also told them stories about people who took charge of their attitudes under challenging circumstances, and shared some powerful quotations. By the time we were finished, they had a much greater understanding of what attitude is and how important it is. They also accepted the fact that attitude is a choice, no matter what the circumstances are.

Everything can be taken from a man but one thing: the last of human freedoms – to choose one's attitude in any given set of circumstances, to choose one's own way.
– Viktor Frankl

By the time we're finished with the lesson on attitude, the students are pretty curious to learn what the other three choices are. Here's the next sign:

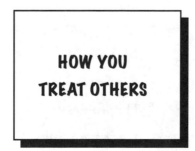

HOW YOU TREAT OTHERS

Remember that on the first day of school we spent most of the class on manners and the Golden Rule. This was the perfect time to reinforce what they learned, and to add something critically important. I told my students that no matter how smart they are and no matter what they achieve, their true success in life will ultimately be determined by their ability to understand and get along with other people. I said, "The better you treat others, the more success you'll have in life."

The importance of treating other people well isn't hard to understand. It sounds good and it sounds like the right thing to do. But it can sometimes be a very challenging choice. I asked them how they would respond in the following scenario: "Let's say you and a small group of friends are eating lunch together out on the campus. Everyone is being polite and you're enjoying one another's company. Then someone who's in a foul mood intrudes upon your group, gets in your face, and says some pretty rude things." The most common answer I received was, "I wouldn't let him get away with it. I'd get right back in his face and let him have it." The truth is that this is the way most people, whether kids or adults, would react under these circumstances.

Then I ask a question: "Who chose your behavior? Did you let the other person make the choice for you by dragging you into the gutter with him? If you do the same thing he's doing by acting rude and obnoxious, you just add fuel to the fire. You make the situation worse. But you do have another choice. You can choose the high road by maintaining your cool and dealing with the situation as politely and calmly as possible. I'm not saying this is an easy choice, especially when someone else is in your face, but it will always be the better choice."

I frequently wrote single words on the board to emphasize the point I was trying to make. In this case, I asked my students to help me out. "What are some of the words that best represent good human relations?" Here are the ones they chose:

Respect	**Manners**	**Courtesy**
Consideration	**Kindness**	**Empathy**
Politeness	**Helpfulness**	**Compassion**
Thoughtfulness	**Understanding**	**Tolerance**
Graciousness	**Friendliness**	**Sincerity**

As I'd done with attitude, I told them stories about people who'd worked hard at developing good social skills, and I shared with them the best quotations I could find on the subject. I added one additional point by putting these words on the board:

We reap what we sow

I asked my students if they'd ever heard of this expression before. Not surprising, some had and some hadn't. I then asked them if they knew where the expression came from. A few said the Bible, and they were right. The passage can be found in the Old Testament in Solomon's Proverbs, and it can be found in the New Testament in Paul's letter to the Galatians. It's one of those Biblical principles that became known as universal truths, whether associated with faith or not. My students had no problem understanding its meaning. Related expressions are "We harvest what we plant," "What you send out comes back to you," and "What goes around, comes around." We eventually pay the price for treating people poorly, and we eventually reap the rewards of treating people with respect and kindness.

> *Our rewards in life will always be in exact proportion*
> *to the amount of consideration we show toward others.*
>
> *– Earl Nightingale*

I told my students, "Just think how far you'll go in life if you always have a good attitude and always show consideration for other people. But you'll go even farther if you make the right choice in the third area." Out came the third sign:

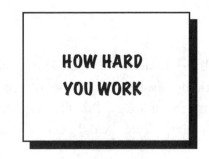

**HOW HARD
YOU WORK**

Many of our students have been led to believe that the nastiest four-lettered word ending in "k" is *work*. Once again I'm referring to the constant barrage of messages from the media that emphasize the "quick and easy" way to getting everything you want out of life. No work, no effort, no sweat, no pain, no sacrifice – just the rewards. So I started this lesson by writing two true-false statements on the board:

All the good things in life come quickly and easily. T F

All the good things in life can be attained without hard work. T F

It's one thing to be bombarded with seductively packaged messages about how to attain "the good life," but it's an entirely different thing to see them in plain English, staring you in the face. I was pleased that all of my students recognized immediately what I was trying to do. They unanimously marked both statements as false, and we had a wonderful discussion about the necessity of hard work in the real world.

As I did with the first two important choices, I added some stories and some quotations about hard work. I closed the lesson by pointing out that hard work and suffering are not the same, and that hard work and fun are not opposites. You can work hard at something and enjoy it at the same time. Teaching is a good example. I found it to be both challenging and difficult work, but the harder I worked at it the more fun I had. The same could be said of people in business, service, the ministry, athletics, or entertainment.

> *I want to be thoroughly used up when I die,*
> *for the harder I work, the more I live.*
>
> *– George Bernard Shaw*

Here's what I said to introduce the final sign: "You'll go far in life if you always have a good attitude, always treat people with respect and kindness, and always work to the best of your ability. But all your achievements and relationships can crumble if you don't make the right choice in one more critical area."

HOW HONEST
YOU ARE

I found teaching about honesty to high school students one of the most difficult tasks I ever took on. Many of our kids are jaded by the time they reach their teenage years. They see so much cheating and lying in our society – in business, athletics, entertainment, and in the government – that many of them conclude that "everyone cheats," and you have to do it also in order to be competitive. They also adopt the philosophy that it's only wrong if you get caught. The saddest part of all of this is that many students tell me their attitudes about cheating begin at home.

I didn't argue that there's not a lot of dishonesty going on in our country, but I did try to convince them of three things:

1 – Not "everyone is doing it." Those who are just get more publicity.

2 – Dishonesty can absolutely ruin lives and relationships.

3 – Honest people have more peaceful, rewarding, and fulfilling lives.

I had them read Chapter 9 in *Life's Greatest Lessons*. It's titled "Honesty is still the best policy." It's one of the most difficult things I've ever written, but it came out the way I hoped it would. My students told me that reading it, hearing my stories, seeing the quotations, doing a questionnaire, and having class discussions all made them examine the whole honesty issue in much greater depth, and it got them to think differently about it. This is the opening paragraph of that chapter:

> *This is the most important chapter in the book. You can do many of the things I suggest here – have a positive attitude, form good habits, laugh, be thankful, set goals, motivate yourself, work hard, be self-disciplined, use time wisely, etc. – but you'll never be truly successful unless everything you do is undergirded with honesty and integrity. You'll never know true peace of mind and you'll never enjoy feelings of self-*

worth unless truthfulness is deeply imbedded in your charat-
er. If you don't learn anything else from reading this book,
it's my most sincere wish and most fervent prayer that you
understand this great truth: honesty always was, is now, and
always will be, the best policy.

One of the other activities that my students found valuable was a simple 10-part questionnaire. Here are the questions:

Is honesty still the best policy?

1 – If you bought any product, from a car to a blender, would you want the salesperson to be honest with you?

2 – If you owned a business, would you want your employees to be honest in dealing with customers and in submitting expense accounts?

3 – If you were riding in a cab, would you want the driver to take the most direct route and charge you fairly?

4 – If you lost your wallet, along with cash, driver's license, and credit cards, would you want the person who found it to return it to you fully intact?

5 – If you invested some of your hard-earned money, would you want the financial adviser to be completely up-front with you?

6 – If you were married or in a serious relationship, would you want your loved one to be honest with you?

7 – If you were competing in an athletic event, would you want the officials and your opponents to conduct themselves honorably?

8 – If you're an employee, do you want your work and achievements to be evaluated fairly, honestly, and on their merits?

9 – If you bought a product with your credit card over the phone or on the Internet, would you want the person handling the transaction to honor your privacy and security?

10 – If you were a recording artist or studio owner, would you want people to buy your music in a legal and honest manner?

It probably won't surprise you that every student answered every question with a "yes" every time I did this exercise. One student made a telling remark. He said, "This is different. No one wants to be ripped off. No one wants to be cheated. These questions are all about when other people do it to us." Then he said, "Oh, now I see what you're getting at." I think all of my students saw what I was getting at. I can't claim that I turned all of them into people of impeccable integrity, but I know I planted some seeds.

> *Honesty is the best policy in international relations, interpersonal relations, labor, business, education, family, and crime control because truth is the only thing that works and the only foundation on which lasting relations can build.*
>
> *– Ramsey Clark*
> *Former U.S. Attorney General*

I mentioned earlier in this chapter that I felt this lesson on life's four most important choices was one of the most important I ever taught. Although I've been out of the classroom for a few years, I'm still asked to speak to students all over the country. The people who hire me always let me select the topic. It's always the same. It's about the four most important choices they'll ever make.

> *We must make the choices that enable us to fulfill the deepest capacities of our real selves.*
>
> *– Thomas Merton*

Good teachers tell good stories

*People are hungry for stories. It's part of our
very being.*

> – Studs Turkel

*Storytelling is the most powerful way to put ideas
into the world today.*

> – Robert McKee

*Stories have power. They delight, enchant, touch,
teach, recall, inspire, motivate, challenge. They
help us understand. They imprint a picture in
our minds. Want to make a point or raise an issue? Tell a story.*

> – Janet Litherland

*Good teaching is often a matter of good storytell-
ing. No matter how high-tech we become, telling
stories to each other orally will endure as one
of our primary and most powerful forms of
communication.*

> – Jason Ohler

A rookie teacher's most valuable lesson

During my first year of teaching I was fortunate to make a friend on the faculty who also became a mentor. He was about eight years older than I, had been teaching for 10 years, and his students absolutely loved him. On a faculty with many outstanding teachers, he was clearly one of the best. It was a real blessing during that challenging first year of teaching to have someone like him to turn to. He always made himself available, was willing to share the most valuable lessons he'd learned about teaching, and often had wonderful advice.

I was only about six weeks into my teaching career when I shared one of my frustrations with him over lunch. I'd just spent several hours on a lesson plan that had completely bombed. He smiled and assured me that this was a normal part of the "rookie experience." Then he asked me a few questions: What was the main point of the lesson? How had I attempted to get that point across? Why did I think the lesson had bombed? I knew it had bombed because my students didn't seem to get it, even though I'd taken great pains to explain it thoroughly. Even worse, they didn't seem to care.

He said, "Maybe your thorough explanation was the problem." This wasn't what I wanted to hear, especially since I was still licking my wounds over all the preparation time that had just gone down the drain. But he continued, "A 'thorough explanation' often comes across to kids as a lecture, and that's a dirty word in their vocabulary. The words most often associated with it are 'boring' and 'deadly.' Most kids will tune out a lecture." Then he paused for a few moments, became a little more animated, and said, "But all kids will listen to a good story. If you want to make a point with them, don't put it in a lecture; put it in a story."

Out of that moment of frustration came one of my greatest lessons as a teacher. I immediately thought about some of the best teachers I'd ever had. Besides loving their jobs and teaching with passion, they were all great storytellers. Dr. Lincoln had made United States history come alive by telling us countless stories and anecdotes about the people who explored and developed our country. Dr. Kirk made English more interesting by telling us fascinating tales about the lives of great literary figures. And Dr. McSweeney left vivid and lasting impressions on his graduate students in education by telling stories about teachers who made a difference in the lives of their students.

One of the most amazing things about good stories is how long they last. Here's a case in point: In November of 2007, when I was about halfway through writing this book, I attended a Character Education conference in Washington, D.C. One of the keynote speakers was Larry Pennie. He's a former teacher who does a marvelous job of imitating Benjamin Franklin – dresses like him, wears his hair like him, and is even shaped like him. He makes his presentation as if he *is* Franklin, telling stories about his life during the early days of our country.

He told about six stories during his keynote address. One of them was about a fictitious character he created while he was working at his brother's print shop. This older brother wouldn't publish any of Franklin's materials because he was "too young." So Franklin wrote articles under the name of Silence Dogood and then slipped them under his brother's office door. They were not only published, but were received with great acclaim by his brother's readers.

I could have told every one of those stories myself. But since I don't look like Benjamin Franklin, I probably wouldn't have been as effective. But I did hold vivid memories of each of his tales. In fact, when he got to the part about getting his writings turned down by his brother, I immediately thought, "Here comes Silence Dogood." How did I know them so well? Had I recently read a biography on Franklin? No. I remembered them from stories Dr. Lincoln had told us in my first college course in U.S. History in the fall of 1959. That was 48 years earlier, and I still remembered the stories as if they'd been told yesterday.

Because I lived in the same community in which I taught, I frequently ran into my students in a variety of local spots. They were both current and former students. It always amused me that my former students, some of them more than 30 years out of high school, wanted to know if I still stood at the door, if I still started class with good news, and if I still told the story about … The completion of that sentence would be the name of a person or an event. The point is that just as I'd remembered Dr. Lincoln's stories, they'd remembered mine.

A good story helps us see the point more clearly
and remember it longer – sometimes forever.

– Professor Erwin G. Hall

Sources for good stories

One of the many things I loved about teaching was working with graduate students in education who were doing their student teaching. I'm sure I had at least 30 student teachers during my career. One of them was a young woman named Jennifer who was getting both her Master's degree and her California Teaching Credential at Stanford University. The plan was for her to observe me for about nine weeks before taking over the teaching of the class for the remainder of the year. At the end of the nine-week observation period, she informed me that she "wasn't quite ready" to step in.

I sensed that she had a little stage fright. I told her it was no problem, and that I'd continue with the class until she was ready. Two more weeks went by, then four, then six. I thought I'd better talk to her again about taking over the class because her professor at Stanford told me he expected her to be teaching by now. Jennifer and I had a little talk in which she informed me that she still "wasn't quite ready." I sensed both anxiety and reluctance, so I asked her what was holding her back. Her answer baffled me. She said, "It's your stories."

I had no idea what she meant. So in mock horror I asked, "What? You don't like my stories?" She said, "I *love* your stories. That's the problem. They're so good and you have so many of them. I don't have any, and the kids will be so disappointed." We had a long talk in which I explained that I didn't think I had any stories either when I started teaching. But the truth is, we all have a lot of great stories in us. The problem is that most schools of education don't emphasize the importance of storytelling as a powerful teaching tool. I also reminded Jennifer that I had more than 25 years of experience before she arrived, and that I'd accumulated a lot of stories along the way.

I also felt a need to help her start developing a supply of stories. Here were the sources I gave her:

- **Personal experiences** – I really believe that by the time a person graduates from college, he or she has hundreds of good stories. We don't think of them at the time they're occurring as potential teaching tools, but that's what they become when we reflect on them later.

- **Family, friends, colleagues, acquaintances** – In other words, people we know. They're a double source of wealth. We can tell stories *about* them and we can tap into the stories they all have to tell.

- **People we read about** – Newspapers, magazines like *Time* and *Newsweek*, and the Internet are full of good stories. They're available to us because they make an important point and they need to be told.

- **Biographies** – I started reading biographies when I was 12 years old. The first one was about Thomas Edison, and it absolutely fascinated me. I was hooked. As a history major in college, I probably read more than a hundred biographies, and I've read even more since then. All of them are full of good stories.

- **Literature** – One of the world's great treasures is the collection of writings by great literary figures. It's so massive we can hardly scratch the surface, so we have a never-ending supply of wonderful stories written by the greatest storytellers of all time. A good example is William Bennett's *The Book of Virtues*. He drew from hundreds of classic pieces of literature that illustrate positive character traits.

- ***Chicken Soup For The Soul*** – There's a good reason why this series of books is so popular and has sold millions of copies. Every book in the series contains short, easy-to-read stories that make important points about the human spirit. I used several of them by either re-telling the story or reading it to my students.

- **Your imagination** – Here's another limitless supply of great stories. Simply put, you can make up stories around the point you want to make with your students. I'm not suggesting that you lie. I'm suggesting that you do the same thing fiction writers do by making up a good story. I did it often. I would begin with, "Let me tell you a good story." It always got my students' attention, and most of the time they didn't bother to ask me whether it was true or not. I don't think they cared. As Studs Terkel says at the opening of this chapter, "People are hungry for stories."

- **Your students** – If you have 20-30 students in your class, you have a lot of good stories. Never underestimate their ability to learn from life experiences or their willingness to share their stories. I would frequently tell a story and then ask my students, "Does anyone else have a story about this?" The answer is frequently yes, and the stories usually reinforce mine.

A few examples of teaching as storytelling

I obviously can't put all my stories into a book of this nature. Even if I could, there are many you'd never want to use simply because they're not *your* stories. But I do want to share a few examples of how I developed a point more fully with the use of a good story. In the previous chapter I wrote about four important choices we need to teach our students: attitude, how we treat others, how hard we work, and how honest we are. Here are a few stories that were part of the lesson on each.

Stories about attitude

First story – Viktor Frankl

Frankl is the author of one of the greatest and most influential books I've ever read, *Man's Search for Meaning*. He was a successful young Jewish physician in Vienna, Austria, in the early 1940s. This was about the time that Adolph Hitler and his Nazi comrades decided to kill every Jew on the face of the earth. Frankl had recently married, and he lived near his parents and his brother. The Nazis took the four of them to one concentration camp and put him in another because he was a doctor. They took away his family, his home, his medical practice, and all his earthly possessions. Then they shaved his head and put a number on his arm. They subjected him and his fellow prisoners to inhumane living conditions and torture while planning to eventually execute them.

Some of Frankl's colleagues committed suicide because they figured that was the only way they could beat the Nazis. Others simply gave up their will to live, got sick, and died before being executed. Frankl was determined to not only survive this horrendous ordeal, but to make a contribution to the world. He thought often about all that the Nazis had taken away from him, and he decided that the only way he could survive was to figure out something they could *never* take away from him.

He came to the conclusion that the last freedom we'll ever have, and one that no one can take away from us, is the freedom to choose one's own attitude, no matter what the circumstances. This is a simple, but profound, concept, and it can be as life-changing for any of us as it was for Frankl. We don't have control over everything that happens to us, but we *do* have control over how we'll deal with what happens. This powerful thought has helped millions of people overcome adversity instead of giving up. Frankl was freed by Allied forces in 1945 and went on to become one of the world's most influential psychotherapists. He left us with a greater understanding of our last freedom.

Second story – Bruce Diaso

I wanted to have another story about attitude that applied Frankl's theory to a different set of circumstances. So I told my students about one of my college classmates. Bruce was a freshman at the University of San Francisco when I was a sophomore. I showed two pictures of him to my students. The first was what we call a "mug shot" from our yearbook. Bruce looks like everyone else in this picture – white shirt, tie, dark sport coat, hair done neatly, big smile. But he looks much different in the second picture. It's a group picture of a club he belonged to. Everyone in the picture is standing except Bruce. He's sitting in his wheelchair.

Bruce was in a wheelchair because he couldn't move either his legs or his arms. He could move his head and neck some, and he could move his hands and fingers, but that was it. He had a normal life until he was a senior in high school, when polio struck. After almost dying in the hospital from it, Bruce was determined to still make something out of his life. And he came to USF with high aspirations. The Dean of Students had organized a cadre of 11 caretakers for Bruce. He lived in a dorm with one of them as his roommate, and the other 10 lived nearby. They not only took care of all his physical needs, they loved and admired Bruce.

It would be safe to say that Bruce was the most respected, admired, and loved student at the university. Why? Did we feel sorry for him because he was paralyzed? That was not the reason. We loved and admired him because he had the greatest attitude of anyone we'd ever known. He was always upbeat, had something positive to say, was courteous and kind to everyone, and he was an outstanding student who worked hard and helped others. And no one ever heard him complain about anything.

Bruce taught me one of the most valuable life lessons I've ever learned. One day he and I were eating lunch together in the dining commons. It was the first time I'd ever been with Bruce without a lot of other people around. I was so fascinated by him I just had to ask him a question about the source of his great attitude. I knew very little about psychology at that time, so I asked Bruce if he was born positive. He smiled and said no. He told me no one is born with a positive attitude, and that he had to work hard to attain his.

Bruce told me that after he got polio he had two dominant feelings – anger and self-pity. He was angry at God and at life because his paralysis was so unfair. He didn't deserve it. He said he felt sorry for himself for several reasons. The main one was that he would never be able to live a normal life. Another one was that he would never be able to play college football. He had been an outstanding high school player. One day his doctor told him, "Bruce, I'd be angry and full of self-pity myself if this had happened to me when I was 17, so I understand how you feel. But you have to ask yourself a question: Are the anger and self-pity making things better for you, or are they making things worse?"

Bruce said he thought about the doctor's question for a long time. He realized that he *was* making things worse, and that he was free to choose another attitude, one that would make things better. So he did. I almost jumped out of my chair. I said, "Bruce, tell me your secret. I want an attitude like yours." He said, "Hal, it's not a secret, and you *can* have an attitude like mine. Anyone can." My next question was obviously one word: "How?" He answered calmly, "Just be thankful for all that you *do* have instead of complaining about what you don't have or what goes wrong. I try to think about all the good people and good things in my life. One of those things is the opportunity to make something out of my life." Like all great ideas, Bruce's was simple: be thankful. Keep in mind that this attitude was his choice. It worked for him and it will work for anyone.

Bruce's success story continued at USF, and he graduated with highest honors in four years. He was awarded a scholarship to law school and graduated from there three years later, again with the highest honors. After turning down many high-paying jobs with law firms, he went back to his hometown of Fresno to become a

Public Defender. He devoted the rest of his life to service to others. Unfortunately, the rest of his life wasn't long enough. He died when he was 31 from complications caused by his paralysis.

Bruce didn't live very long, and he lived all of his short adult life paralyzed and in a wheelchair. But he touched everyone who knew him in a positive and loving way. And he's touched countless other lives since he died in 1972 because his friends continue to tell his story, especially about his attitude.

Stories about how we treat others

There are some wonderful stories about people like Abraham Lincoln, Mohandas Gandhi, Albert Schweitzer, and Mother Teresa that inspire us to treat other people with compassion. I often used them as excellent examples of kindness and its rewards. But I also had a few stories that were more personal.

One of them was about Tim Hansel, a colleague of mine for one magical year back in the early 1970s. I mentioned Tim in Chapter 8. And because of the impact he's had on my life, I've mentioned him in all of my books. Maybe you have someone in your life that seems to always bring sunshine as Tim did. If you do, tell your students about him or her. Stories about personal friends and what they do for us can be powerful.

The thing I emphasize the most in my stories about Tim is his ability to bring out the best in others. You may recall that I wrote earlier about this as being the No. 1 mission of a parent or teacher. Tim did it better than anyone I've ever known. He looked for the good in other people, he found it, and then he told them what he found. His favorite question was, "Do you know what I like the most about you?" Believe me, everyone wants to hear the answer.

I've also told many stories about my mother, Ruth Urban. She's 94 as I write this, and just as aware, kind, and considerate as she's ever been. Everyone loves her for a simple reason. Whether she's dealing with a family member, an old friend, or a new acquaintance, she puts the other person's needs and interests first. She's a perfect example of reaping what she sows. Maybe one or both of your parents is like this. If so, there are some good stories to tell, and because they're personal, they'll have an impact.

Stories about hard work

There are probably more stories about persistence, determination, and hard work than any other topic. Maybe it all started with *The Little Engine That Could*, or maybe it started earlier, but stories about hard work abound. Because the first biography I ever read was about Thomas Edison, I frequently told stories about his legendary work ethic. It was Edison who said, "Genius is one percent inspiration and 99 percent perspiration." When asked how he could keep working on a project after it had failed to work more than 10,000 times, he would reply that he hadn't failed. Each effort that didn't work brought him closer to the one that did.

My favorite story regarding hard work is about Francisco Rivera. He's a gardener in my hometown of Redwood City, California. Francisco and his wife Lydia and their three children came here from Mexico in the early 1980s. He spoke no English and had very little money. Their first home here could best be described as a shack. I came to know the family because my wife Cathy and I belonged to a small group at our church, and we were involved in the "Adopt-A-Family" program at Christmas time. We adopted the Rivera family, which meant we were going to buy them some food, clothing, and toys for the children.

Lydia spoke some English, so all of my early interactions with the family were through her. She told me she had turned her family's name in to the church because they had so little while trying to get started in this country. Francisco didn't want to accept "handouts" or "welfare" because he wanted to support his own family. He came to the United States because it was "the land of opportunity." Through Lydia, I convinced him that this was neither a handout nor welfare. I asked him to look upon it as a one-time Christmas gift. He accepted under those conditions. They were very appreciative of all we did for them.

A year later I received a call from Lydia. She asked if I knew anything about buying a home. I told her I knew a little because I had bought my first home, and six years later sold it and bought a larger one. She said they were interested in buying a home. I didn't want to discourage her, but the area we live in south of San Francisco is one of the most expensive in the country. They couldn't possibly have enough money for a down payment after only one year in the country. A year earlier Francisco didn't speak English and hadn't yet started his gardening business.

Lydia told me that Francisco had worked very hard, that the gardening business was doing well, and that they had saved a lot of money. She said Francisco was making more than $6,000 per month. I was sure she had meant $600 per month and that she didn't realize how expensive homes were in our area. He couldn't possibly have made that much money in his first year in the country. But I did as she requested and hooked her up with a friend of mine who sold real estate. He called me later and said, "This Francisco guy is unbelievable! He doesn't make $6,000 per month – he makes $6,500 per month." He made $78,000 in his first year in the country. Keep in mind that this was back in the early 1980s. They had, indeed, saved enough money for a down payment, and they bought a home.

I met with Francisco later because I wanted to know more about how all of this happened. I also told him that I loved to tell stories and that I wanted to tell his, especially to my students. He said, "Señor Urban, please tell your students that there's no substitute for hard work. There's no 'quick and easy' way. There's only hard work. I came here knowing that if I worked hard it would pay off, and it has. I not only do the best job possible, but always do something a little extra. The men who work for me know this is the standard I have, so they do the same. My customers are always happy with the work we do, and they recommend us to all their friends. We now do the gardening at many large homes and businesses, and the business is still growing. It's all because of hard work."

Stories about honesty

There are plenty of heroic stories about how people of different ages chose to be honest even when they knew they could get away with something that would greatly enrich them in a material sense. I've told many of those stories, always with the emphasis on the rewards of integrity – inner peace, a solid reputation, trust, self-esteem, a sense of wholeness, and joy. But there's something else that I think works better.

In the previous chapter I shared 10 questions that I asked my students about honesty. They got the point, and we had a wonderful discussion afterwards. And they all had stories of their own about times when someone was dishonest with them. This always seemed to work more effectively than an idealistic story, at least in this case, because it brought the issue closer to home.

Conclusion: What good stories accomplish

Many people don't realize the extent to which stories influence our behavior and even shape our culture. Think about how Bible stories teach the fundamentals of religion and rules of conduct. Think of the fables and parables that molded your values. Think of how stories about your national, cultural, or family history have shaped your attitudes about yourself and others.

– Lawrence Shapiro
How to Raise a Child With a High EQ

If stories come to you, care for them. And learn to give them away where they are needed. Sometimes a person needs a story more than food to stay alive.

– Barry Lopez

Stories are the creative conversion of life itself into a more powerful, clearer, more meaningful experience. They are the currency of human contact.

– Robert McKee

Stories live in your blood and bones, follow the seasons and light candles on the darkest night. Every storyteller knows he or she is also a teacher.

– Patti Davis

Good teachers use the power of quotations

I love quotations because it is a joy to find thoughts one might have, beautifully expressed with much authority, by someone recognized as wiser than myself.

– Marlene Dietrich

Wise sayings help teachers make their point

I quote others only in order the better to express myself.

– Michel De Montaigne

I've never known anyone who doesn't appreciate a good quotation. Even people who aren't fond of reading seem to enjoy and value them. No one appreciates them more than teachers and authors. Good quotations, along with good stories, help us give extra credence to the points we're trying to make. Using a quotation is like saying, "See, here's proof. Look at what this wise person has to say about the same topic."

Most teachers do a lot of reading beyond their students' papers, as in newspapers, magazines, and books. We discover early on that wise and concise statements by other people not only seem to jump out at us, but have staying power. Sometimes we can read a brief statement only once, and because it's so insightful and powerful, it becomes etched in our minds forever. My best teachers, besides telling good stories, always seemed to have an appropriate quotation to accompany their lessons. And every good book I've ever read includes quotations from other authors.

I used quotations throughout my teaching career, and if you've read any of my four previous books, you know that I use them extensively in my writing. My editors at Simon & Schuster frequently suggested that I had too many quotations. But I reminded them that my readers were constantly thanking me for the "great quotations" included in my books, so they stayed in. Those readers probably liked the quotations more than they did my writing. But that's OK, because I do, too. My third book, *Choices That Change Lives*, has more than 325 quotations in it. You'll probably love the book even if you skip what I wrote and just read the quotations.

I've always believed that all the great observations about human nature and behavior were written down long ago. That's the wonder of a great quotation. We marvel at some wise person's ability to make a statement of great meaning and impact while using only a few words. The beauty of these quotations is that they crystallize important ideas for us. They're short, get right to the point, are full of common sense and wisdom, and are easy to remember. We treasure the insight expressed in these simple maxims, and we can't resist sharing them with others. That's why they can be such powerful teaching tools.

> *There are single thoughts that contain the essence of a whole volume, single sentences that have the beauties of a larger work.*
>
> – Joseph Joubert

The best sources for quotations

Back in the old days, finding good quotations was a lot of hard work. You had to get a copy of *Bartlett's Familiar Quotations* or scour several books in the library. You could hunt for just the right quotation for hours and still not come up with it. I experienced this frustration several times when I was writing the first edition of *Life's Greatest Lessons* in 1990. Yes, 1990 was in the old days, which means before the Internet. The search engines that came with it kept getting better and better, meaning there finally was a "quick and easy" way to do something. Then along came Google, making it even quicker and easier. But that isn't the only source of good quotations, so let me make a few recommendations:

1 – Books devoted entirely to quotations – These are still valuable and reliable sources. While *Bartlett's* is the standard bearer, there are many other that are helpful. I own more than 20 books of quotations, and I refer to them often. Many of them were gifts from students. They not only loved my quotations, but they also wanted to make sure that I never ran out of them. All teachers should own at least a few of these valuable resources. Some books of quotations now focus on particular themes. A good recent example is *Character Quotations* by Tom Lickona and Matt Davidson. I have others that focus on success, leadership, relationships, virtues, and humor. An Internet search will help you find what you want.

2 – Other books – This may be a little slower, but still valuable. We've all read books that are so good they become like old friends. We visit them frequently and are renewed each time we do. It's worth the time you spend hunting for the pearls of wisdom contained in these books.

3 – Other people, especially colleagues – Because so many people, especially educators, appreciate quotations, you can always tap into their supplies. Everyone likes to share their favorite quotations. I have a lot of literate friends, both in and out of education, who not only supplied me with excellent quotations, but with good book recommendations as well.

4 – The Internet – This is a quotation lover's paradise. You go to Google, type in "quotes about character," (or any other topic) and you'll find more than you can use. The hardest part is reading through so many to find just the right one. This does come with a warning, however. Some of the people who post quotations on the Internet get a little sloppy. Some of the quotations are worded incorrectly and some of them are attributed to the wrong person. When you find one you're going to use, I suggest that you double and triple check it with other sources.

> *Most collectors collect tangibles. As a quotation collector, I collect wisdom, life, invisible beauty, souls alive in ink.*
>
> *– Terri Guillemets*

> *Collecting quotations is an insidious, even embarrassing habit, like rag picking or hoarding rocks or trying on other people's laundry. I got into it originally while trying to break an addiction to candy. I kicked candy and now seem to be stuck with quotations, which are attacking my brain instead of my teeth.*
>
> *– Robert Byrne*

Some favorite quotations about some favorite topics

You'll recall that a few chapters back (14) I wrote about the importance of helping young people see the choices they have and helping them make good ones. You'll also recall that I think the four most important choices we make have to do with attitude, how we treat others, how hard we work, and how honest we are. In the previous chapter, I shared some of the stories I used in teaching those lessons. I also mentioned that I used quotations to add to the stories. The rest of this chapter contains some of the quotations I used along with the stories.

In addition to quotations pertaining to the four most important choices, I've included some other virtues that I did my best to teach along with some of the quotations I used.

Attitude

Our attitudes propel us forward toward our victories or bog us down in defeat. They are the foothold beneath us in every step we take. They are what others see most of the personality within us; they describe us and define us, projecting the image we present to the world around us. Our attitudes make us rich or poor, happy or unhappy, fulfilled or incomplete. They are the single most determining factor in every action we will ever make. We and our attitudes are inextricably combined; we are our attitudes and our attitudes are us.

– Shad Helmstetter

The longer I live, the more I realize the impact of attitude on life. Attitude, to me, is more important than facts. It is more important than the past, than education, than money, than circumstances, than failures, than successes, than what other people think or say or do. It is more important than appearance, giftedness or skill. It will make or break a company … a church … a home. The remarkable thing is we have a choice every day regarding the attitude we will embrace for that day. We cannot change our past … we cannot change the fact that people will act in a certain way. We cannot change the inevitable. The only thing we can do is play on the one string we have, and that is our attitude. I am convinced that life is 10 percent what happens to me and 90 percent how I react to it. And so it is with you. We are in charge of our attitudes.

– Charles Swindoll

Attitude is everything.
– Keith Harrell

How we treat others

Treat other people exactly as you would like to be treated by them.

— Matthew 7:12

Kind words are short and easy to speak, but their echoes are truly endless.

— Mother Teresa

You have to sow before you can reap. You have to give before you can get.

— Robert Collier

Service to others is the rent we pay for living on this planet.

— Marian Wright Edelman

No kind action ever stops with itself. One kind action leads to another. Good example is followed. A single act of kindness throws out roots in all directions, and the roots spring up and make new trees. The greatest work that kindness does to others is that it makes them kind themselves.

— Amelia Earhardt

Love and kindness are never wasted. They always make a difference. They bless the one who receives them, and they bless you, the giver.

— Barbara DeAngelis

Kindness is the golden chain by which society is bound together.

— Goethe

How hard we work

The best prize life offers is the chance to work hard at work worth doing.

– Theodore Roosevelt

If you are called to be a street sweeper, sweep streets even as Michelangelo painted, or Beethoven composed music, or Shakespeare wrote poetry. Sweep streets so well that all the hosts of heaven and earth will pause to say, "Here lived a great street sweeper who did his job well."

– Martin Luther King, Jr.

The harder I work, the luckier I get.

– Samuel Goldwyn

True happiness comes to him who does his work well, followed by a relaxing and refreshing period of rest. True happiness comes from the right amount of work for the day.

– Lin Yu–T'ang

I want to be thoroughly used up when I die, for the harder I work, the more I live.

– George Bernard Shaw

I know the price of success: dedication, hard work, and an unremitting devotion to the things you want to see happen.

– Frank Lloyd Wright

There is no substitute for hard work.

– Thomas Edison

How honest we are

Honesty is the first chapter in the book of wisdom.

> *– Thomas Jefferson*

Each time you are honest and conduct yourself with honesty, a success force will drive you toward greater success. Each time you lie, even with a little white lie, there are strong forces pushing you toward failure.

> *– Joseph Sugarman*

Honesty is the best policy. If I lose mine honor, I lose myself.

> *– William Shakespeare*

Honesty is the cornerstone of all success, without which confidence and ability to perform shall cease to exist.

> *– Mary Kay Ash*

Only a life of goodness and honesty leaves us feeling spiritually healthy and human.

> *– Rabbi Harold Kushner*

The great rewards of being an honest person are peace of mind, a good reputation, relationships built on trust, a sense of wholeness, self-respect, and a feeling of authenticity.

> *– Professor Erwin G. Hall*

A life lived with integrity - even if it lacks the trappings of fame and fortune – is a shining star in whose light others may follow in the years to come.

> *– Denis Waitley*

Opportunity

The golden opportunity you are seeking is in yourself. It is not in your environment; it is not in luck or chance, or the help of others; it is in yourself alone.

– Orison Swett Marden

Opportunity is all around us. If we seek it, we will find it. And if the door of opportunity is closed, we must knock on it – and keep on knocking until it opens.

– Wynn Davis

In the middle of difficulty lies opportunity.

– Albert Einstein

Possibilities

You have powers you never dreamed of. You can do things you never thought you could do. There are no limitations in what you can do except the limitations of your own mind.

– Darwin P. Kingsley

Everyone has inside of him a piece of good news. The good news is that you don't know how great you can be! How much you can love! What you can accomplish! And what your potential is!

– Anne Frank

If we did all the things we are capable of doing, we would literally astound ourselves.

– Thomas Edison

Motivation

No matter who you are or what your age may be, if you want to achieve permanent, sustaining success, the motivation that will drive you toward that goal must come from within.

– Paul J. Meyer

Motivation starts with a sense of desire. ... When you want something, you become motivated to get it.

– Denis Waitley

The potential for major increases in achievement and self-development exists in everyone, and the starting point is an internal decision to excel.

– Charles Garfield

Success

Success means doing the best we can with what we have. Success is in the doing, not the getting – in the trying, not the triumph. Success is a personal standard – reaching for the highest that is in us – becoming all that we can be. If we do our best, we are a success.

– Wynn Davis

Successful people understand the difference between existing and living, and always choose the latter. They get the most out of life because they put the most into it. They reap what they sow. And they enjoy life to the fullest.

– Professor Erwin G. Hall

My all-time favorites

If I were asked to give what I consider the single most useful bit of advice for all humanity it would be this: Expect trouble as an inevitable part of life and when it comes, hold your head high, look it squarely in the eye, and say, "I will be bigger than you. You cannot defeat me."

– Ann Landers

*I understand **The Courage to Be** as the courage to say "yes" to life in spite of all the negative elements in human existence – in spite of man's finitude, which means his coming from nothing, and going to nothing, to die. Man's guilt and fear, because he is estranged from what he truly is and what he truly ought to be, involves his anxiety about losing the meaning of his life.*

In spite of all this which the man of our time experiences so deeply, it means the courage to say "yes" to life, because life has an ultimate meaning, and I will live and actualize it. It takes courage to see in the reality around us and in us something ultimately positive and meaningful and live with it, even love it. Loving life is perhaps the highest form of the courage to be.

– Paul Tillich

Good teachers laugh with their students

*Research has consistently shown that good teach-
ers have a sense of humor, and they are able to
use humor as part of their teaching methods.
Humor, used properly, can be a powerful addition
to any lesson.*

– Bob Kizlik

Another critically important quality

You may recall that way back in the first chapter I wrote about the single most important quality of a successful teacher – enthusiasm. Good teachers love what they do, they find a certain joy in it, and they have a lot of fun (at least most of the time). There's another quality that ties in with all of this, and I would rank it second only to enthusiasm in importance. It's a good sense of humor. Not only is it essential for effective teaching, it's an absolute necessity for both your sanity and your survival.

Teaching is one of the most demanding and stressful jobs in existence. The most effective coping device we have is laughter. There's now a mountain of scientific evidence that proves laughter is a stress reducer. It can also enhance respiration, produce morphine-like molecules called endorphins, increase the number of disease-fighting immune cells, lessen pain, stimulate the internal organs, and improve blood circulation.

In other words, laughter contributes to good health, and no one needs it more than a teacher.

I'm not saying that you have to be as clever or as funny as Robin Williams, Whoopi Goldberg, or Jerry Seinfeld. If you were, you'd be out making people laugh from a stage or behind a TV camera, and making a lot more money than you do. But you can still bring a lot of humor into your school or classroom. I'm not a naturally funny person who can come up with a quick one-liner every time someone says something, but there are other ways to make students laugh. Humor was always an essential part of my strategy for connecting with students. Remember, "If you can reach 'em, you can teach 'em." A variation of that old saying is, "If you can get them to laugh, you can get them to learn."

Laughter is the shortest distance between two people.

– Victor Borge

The best sources for humor in the classroom

Humor aligns the students and teacher and links them through enjoyment. When people laugh together, they become united.

– Professor Robert Provine

Let me give you fair warning that finding good humor for the classroom is far more difficult and time-consuming that finding good stories or quotations. To begin with, what we think is funny might not be so funny to our students. It also works the other way around – they often laugh at things we don't find amusing. So step number one is finding out what they think is funny. A first-grader and a 12th-grader won't laugh at the same thing because a sense of humor develops in stages. It's our job to find out which stage our students are in and what makes them laugh.

The most important thing to do when you hear or see something funny that will work with your students is to write it down and put it in a location reserved just for humor. If you don't write it down it will fade from your memory very quickly. Teaching does that to our brains. If you write it down but don't put it in a special place, you'll probably lose it. Teaching does that to our brains also. One of my constant traveling companions is a thick orange folder. All it says on the tab is "Humor." I often hold it up at speaking engagements and point out to teachers that it was one of my most valuable possessions. In it are my notes and copies of jokes, one-liners, short stories, anecdotes, letters, advertisements, newspaper headlines, church bulletins, signs, and anything else I could find that made me laugh. Actually, the orange humor folder I carry with me is No. 6 in the series. The first one started during the 1967-68 school year. This one started during the 1998-99 school year. Altogether, they contain a 35-year collection of humor that works in the classroom. Yes, it might be my next book. Based on my experiences, these are the most valuable sources of humor:

- **Books** – You'll probably find this hard to believe, but I own 48 books devoted entirely to humor. I thought I had about 20, but for the sake accuracy I counted them before writing this paragraph. Some are excellent and some are a joke – a bad one. While the good ones contain a lot of humor, the process of finding it is a slow one. You'll have to read several jokes, anecdotes, stories, one-liners, etc., in order to find the one or two gems you'll be able to use. But if you're willing to put in the hours, it will pay off. It's also a pleasant way to spend time.

- **The Internet** – Just as you can do a Google search for quotations, you can do one for humor. Here are a few of the key phrases to type into the search area: clean humor, clean jokes, jokes for school, children's humor, and one-liners. Again, it will take some time, but you'll have fun doing it, and you'll end up with some valuable material. It's also a lot cheaper than buying all those books.

- **Your eyes and ears and a pencil** – This, I believe, is the best way to find humor. Be on the lookout for it everywhere you go. There's an old expression that tells us we always find what we're looking for. There's humor all around us on most days. Look for it, listen for it, and when you find it, write it down and then put it in a folder or notebook or some other place designated just for humor.

Here's a simple example of finding humor in the unexpected. My wife Cathy and I were driving from Phoenix to Tucson several years ago. Along the highway we came upon a sign put up by the state of Arizona. It read in large letters at the top, "STATE PRISON AHEAD." A little bit further down, on the same sign, were these words: "Do not stop for hitchhikers." I thought it was hilarious. I wanted to get out and add, "Especially if they're in orange jump suits." But some other people in our group who also saw it didn't find anything humorous about it. I guess they were concentrating on the road.

- **Television** – Despite the overall low quality of programs on TV, there are still some good ones, and some of them are sitcoms. While only a small percentage of the funny lines you hear on TV are useful at school, they're still worth making a note of. Keep in mind that they're written by professional comedy writers. There are also a number of stand-up comedians who appear on a variety of TV shows who provide some good laughs. The stand-ups on HBO and other pay channels, however, are usually too crude to provide you with anything you can use at school.

- **Your funny friends** – We all have some of these wonderful people in our lives. They remind us to not take ourselves too seriously. They also remind us how important it is to laugh. While we may not be as funny as they are, they're a good source of humor. For instance, I have a friend who makes up funny phrases that don't make any sense. One of his favorites is, "Get a neck!" I don't say that to other people, but I tell them about my crazy friend who does, and I always get a laugh out of it. I have another friend who does the Superman call. For you younger people who didn't grow up on Superman, here was the call: "Look, it's a bird! No, it's a plane! No, it's Superman! Up, up, and away!" Maybe you don't think it's funny. But it was when my friend said it because he said it backwards. It came out like this: "Kool, s'ti a dirb! On, s'ti a enalp! On, s'ti namrepus! Pu, pu, dna yawa!" Try saying that without laughing.

- **Your students** – Back in Chapter 9, I explained what we did at the beginning of each class. To refresh your memory (which I'm sure is on overload by now), after I greeted my students at the door and took roll, I pointed to the "CELEBRATE TODAY!" sign and asked them who had something good to share. They had four choices: good news, something or someone they were thankful for, kind words about someone in the class, or something funny. Two students each day were assigned to "Laughter Detail." Two restrictions: cannot be dirty and cannot be mean-spirited. Once they got going they discovered there were all types of sources out there for good, clean humor. They came up with good jokes, told hilarious stories and did wacky things. It nourished the atmosphere of the class and it took a lot of pressure off of me to come up with something funny every day.

> *Kids of all ages and all cultural backgrounds love to act silly, say funny things, and laugh. Teachers need to understand that they need to be able to do this in school, too.*
>
> *– Professor Joseph Napier*

Some of my favorites

People collect all kinds of things – coins, stamps, dolls, cars, works of art, wines, pins, money (no teachers on this one), and a countless variety of "things." I collect books, quotations, and humor. At the end of my previous four books, I've shared some of my own favorite books with my readers. In the last chapter I shared some of my favorite quotations among the thousands in my collection. It's now time to share some of my favorite funnies with you. I hope you get a laugh out of them, and I hope you'll use them to make others laugh.

Because these are among my favorites, I often use them when I speak. So if you've heard me speak, they might sound familiar to you. But they'll still be funny. Also, if you've heard me speak you'll know that my favorite type of humor is what I call "unintended and unexpected" It's when people *aren't* trying to be funny, but things they say or write just happen to come out funny:

- Several years ago a little girl in the fifth grade wrote a letter to me regarding my first book, *Life's Greatest Lessons*, which was then called *20 Things I Want My Kids to Know*. She and her classmates had read it over a period of months under the guidance of their teacher. This is how she closed her letter: "I think I've become a better person since we read your book, and my mother thinks so, too. She is very nice and pretty and single. Are you married?" When I wrote back to the class I put a little note in for her. I told her that it was sweet of her to look out for her mom that way. There were just two problems – one, I was a little too old for her mother, and second, I was a little too married.

- During one of the many years that I taught a course called World Cultures to ninth-graders, I got a surprise and a chuckle while correcting tests. We had spent a lot of time on "The Age of Exploration," so my students were pretty familiar with names like Christopher Columbus, Ferdinand Magellan, Vasco de Gama, and several others. The first question on the test was the easiest: "What is Ferdinand Magellan's most famous achievement?" One of my students knew what Magellan did, but he got a word mixed up. His answer: "He was the first person to circumcise the world." I gave him credit.

- When I was doing my student-teaching, another student did something similar on a U.S. History test regarding the Civil War. We had spent much time talking about the greatness of Abraham Lincoln, so once again, the easiest question was at the beginning of the test: "What was the name of the famous document President Lincoln signed that was intended to end slavery in the U.S. forever?" This student also knew the answer, but he got a word mixed up: "The Emancipation Constipation." I gave him credit.

- A church I used to attend had several small groups for people in all stages of life. One of them was for new mothers. It was called The Little Mothers Club. An announcement in the church bulletin looked like this:

Little Mothers Club Meets Wednesday Evening

"Any ladies in the church interested in becoming a Little Mother should see the pastor in his study." Such announcements need to be worded more carefully.

- Also from a church bulletin: "Ladies, don't forget the rummage sale. It's a chance to get rid of those things not worth keeping around the house. Don't forget to bring your husbands."

- Sign near the highway in Indiana at a combination diner/gas station: "EAT HERE AND GET GAS"

- From the classified ads: "Leaving the country, must part with wonderful dog – doberman pincher – smart, young, strong, good guard dog, eats anything, loves children."

- Also from the classified ads: "Antique desk – suitable for lady with thick legs and big drawers."

- My favorite bumper sticker: "HONK IF YOU LOVE PEACE AND QUIET"

- Sentence completion exercise with fourth-graders: "An idle mind is … the best way to relax." "Better be safe than … punch a fifth-grader."

- International marketing blunder: Frank Perdue, who was famous in Maryland for selling chickens for barbecuing, had the slogan, "It takes a strong man to make a tender chicken." When the slogan was translated into Spanish, it came out, "It takes an aroused man to make a chicken affectionate."

- A note from one of my students' mother after an absence: "Maryanne was absent on Tuesday because she had a fever and upset stomach. Her sister was also sick, and her brother had a fever. I wasn't too well, either. There must be something going around. Her father even got hot last night."

- Sign on a church marquee: "If you're tired of sin, come on in." A few days later someone added: "If you're not, call 366-9882."

Laughter is the sun that drives winter from the human face.

– Victor Hugo

Remember that children laugh an average of 146 times a day; adults laugh an average of four times a day. Put more laughter in your day.

– Dorfus Chucklepants

Good teachers inspire their students to set goals

Many people fail in life, not for lack of ability or brains or even courage, but simply because they have never organized their energies around a goal.

– Elbert Hubbard

People with goals succeed because they know where they're going.

– Earl Nightingale

Why students of all ages should be taught to set goals

Back in the early 1980s a professor at the University of South Carolina, John N. Gardner, started a program on campus called "The Freshman Year Experience." He was appalled by the number of students who don't adjust well to college in their first year and end up dropping or flunking out. He and his colleagues searched for the reasons and for solutions to the problem. They discovered that one of the main causes was lack of direction. The freshmen having the most problems had never been taught anything about setting goals, either for the short term or for a lifetime.

The program addressed this issue, along with several others, and was highly successful in raising the retention rate of first-year college students. It then spread to other colleges throughout the country and eventually became an international success. One of my colleagues at the University of San Francisco was deeply involved and claimed it was the best thing universities had done for freshmen in the 30-plus years he had been a professor.

He said, "The best thing we do is help these kids set goals for themselves. It's too bad this is the first time that most of them have even *thought* about having goals, let alone be taught about the process of setting them." I told him that I'd been teaching my high school students to set goals for many years, and that I loved doing it. He responded, "You're a rare bird. More than 98 percent of our students have never been taught anything about setting goals." He went on to say that even if all our students *were* learning to set goals in high school, it wouldn't be early enough. He felt very strongly that all schools, starting with students as young as the first grade, should be helping kids learn to set goals. He said, "Goal-setting should be taught early, and it should be reinforced, refined, and expanded every succeeding year in school. Just think how much more direction our kids would have if they went through this process. Even the kids who don't go to college would benefit greatly." He only confirmed what I had believed for many years.

> *Man is a goal-seeking animal. His life only has meaning if he is reaching out and striving for his goals.*
>
> *– Aristotle*

> *You got to be careful if you don't know where you're going, because you might not get there.*
>
> *– Yogi Berra*

Teaching kids to motivate themselves through their goals

Motivation is probably one of the most misunderstood words in the English language. I think the main reason is that so many people think motivation comes from something or someone outside themselves. Athletes expect their coaches to motivate them, businesspeople want their bosses to motivate them, and many parents are hoping that teachers will motivate their kids. But the truth is that real motivation is an inside job. Motivation comes from the word *motive,* which, according to *Webster's Dictionary,* is "that within the individual, rather than without, which causes him or her to act." In other words, all of our actions have motives, or reasons. They come from needs felt deeply inside. And no one else can fill them for us. This is why the title of Chapter 11 in *Life's Greatest Lessons* is "Real motivation comes from within." I didn't try to motivate my students – I tried to inspire them. There's a difference. I taught them what real motivation is and I taught them to motivate themselves by writing goals.

> *No matter who you are or what your age may be, if you want to achieve permanent, sustaining success, the motivation that will drive you toward that goal must come from within.*
>
> – Paul J. Meyer

This is the quotation I used to open the lesson on goal-setting. I'd also like to share with you something I wrote at the beginning of the chapter on goal-setting in my first book: "There's a good reason why the chapter on goals follows the one on motivation. Together, they're not only the greatest source of human power, but the seeds of all success. When we combine motivation with our goals, there's hardly anything that can stop us. All achievements, no matter how great or small, are ignited as goals and fueled through motivation. Goals not only encompass all of life, but are the most effective self-motivators we can have. The goals we set and the depth of our motivation will determine, more than anything else, what we make of our lives."

*Goals are not only absolutely necessary to motivate us,
they are essential to keeping us alive.*

– Robert H. Schuller

The most enjoyable and valuable lesson I ever taught

I can't possibly put into words how much fun I had teaching my students about goal-setting. But I wasn't the only one having fun. Most of my students not only thoroughly enjoyed writing goals, they told me afterward that it was one of the most valuable things they ever did in school. And of all the things I taught, goal-setting is by far the subject I receive the most feedback on. I still hear from students I taught more than 30 years ago about their goals – the ones that have been achieved, the ones that have been added since they were in my class, and the ones they're still working on. Nothing is more gratifying to a teacher than to learn that something he or she taught had a positive and lasting influence.

While writing this book I heard from five of my former students regarding the goals they wrote in my class. Two of them are now teachers, one is an airline pilot, one is a lawyer, and one is in medical school. They always remind me that I told them to write down their goals, to look at them every day, and to visualize themselves achieving them. They said they could still hear me saying, "It's not a goal unless you use this process to burn it into your mind."

I also heard from a 53-year-old man who read the chapter on goal-setting in *Life's Greatest Lessons*. He told me that he had wanted to go into the Peace Corps since he was in college, but kept putting it off. He got into the sales of medical supplies and earned a good salary, putting off the Peace Corps even longer. He said a few years ago a friend had given him the book, and after reading it, two chapters seemed to stick with him. Chapter 1 is "Success is more than making money," and Chapter 12 is "Goals are dreams with deadlines." His letter came to me from Peru, where he is now in the Peace Corps and working on another one of his goals – learn to speak Spanish. It's nice to know that teaching can extend beyond the classroom and to people of all ages.

Teaching the process – setting goals is more than wishing

Although someone else may do it differently, I'd like to share with you the seven-step process I used to teach my students about goal-setting:

1 – Assignment: Write 10 lifetime goals

2 – Define what goals are; distinguish between goals and non-goals

3 – Develop categories of goals

4 – Tell the story of John Goddard and his goals

5 – Share some of my own goals and stories

6 – Teach the 15 principles of effective goal-setting

7 – Assignment: Write 100 lifetime goals

I started the lesson by asking my students how many of them had ever been taught to set goals. None. Then I announced that I was giving them an assignment to write down 10 lifetime goals. The first time I did this I was naïve. I thought all the students would find it to be easy and fun. Not so. Many of them thought 10 were too many. They hadn't really done much life planning yet. After all, they were "still in high school." I still remember the first comment I ever heard when giving this assignment. One of the boys in the class who had somewhat of a negative outlook on life asked in a sarcastic tone, "How are we supposed to know what we want to do 20 years from now?" I responded with a smile and said, "Well, there's a lot of evidence that people with goals achieve far more with their lives and are happier than those without goals. Do you think it would be worth exploring?" My comment got the students' attention, and almost all of them responded favorably.

My next step was to use a good quotation, one of my favorites on goal-setting:

> *Life takes on meaning when you become motivated,*
> *set goals, and charge after them in an unstoppable*
> *manner.*
> *– Les Brown*

Following a great discussion, I handed out the following assignment:

Date_____ Name _____

GOALS

List below 10 things you'd like to achieve in your lifetime. Write down only those that you honestly believe you can accomplish.

1) _____

2) _____

3) _____

4) _____

5) _____

6) _____

7) _____

8) _____

9) _____

10) _____

Which one of these is the most important to you? _____

Why? _____

_____

_____

Defining what a goal is

This second step was done after the students turned in their list of goals. I was deliberately vague when I gave the assignment. No one asked me what a goal was, so I concluded that everyone had at least some idea. After they turned in their papers, I told them I was going to make two lists on the board from their papers. The first list would be goals and the second list would be non-goals. I said, "Don't get mad if one of the goals you wrote appears in the non-goal list. There's a reason why I did it this way. Besides, we can change all the non-goals into goals."

Here's an example of what the lists looked like:

Goals	Non-Goals
Play baseball in college	Make more than enough money
Get a job in fashion design	Become very educated
Get accepted to UCLA	Become famous for a good reason
Go to Italy	Travel extensively
Become a dentist	Have good social skills
Own a Mustang	Lead an exciting life
Learn to speak fluent Spanish	Give a donation to a worthy cause
See "Cats" on Broadway	Be happy and well off
Read *War and Peace*	Have success in my career
See a Super Bowl game	Lose a lot of weight
Run a mile in under 5:00	Live in my dream house
Visit all 50 states	Be a writer
Build a home in Tucson	Enjoy life to the max

By looking at the two lists you can easily figure out why some are goals and some are not. Most of my students picked it up as soon as I completed putting the lists on the board. You'll notice the ones on the left are specific. The student who wrote each of them will know exactly when the goal has been achieved. The ones on the right are too vague to be goals. There's not a real target the student is aiming for, so there won't be any specific time at which he or she can say, "I achieved my goal." Some of them can become goals by making them more specific. Some of them cannot be turned into goals. Everyone wants to be happy, well off, and enjoy life to the max, but those aren't goals.

Here are a few examples of turning non-goals into goals:

Non-goal: Become very educated

Goal: Earn a Bachelor's, Master's, and Doctorate in history

Non-goal: Travel extensively

Goal: Visit at least three countries in Europe, Africa, and Asia

Non-goal: Lose a lot of weight

Goal: Lose 40 pounds in the next 12 months

Non-goal: Be a writer

Goal: Write children's books for a profession, or Write for *Sports Illustrated* magazine

Small children will write goals that are much less specific than middle school and high school students. That's OK. The idea is to get them started and to help them refine their goals as they get older and understand more about the world.

I realized when I started teaching the goal-setting process in the early 1970s that it would be helpful for both my students and me if we were all operating from the same definition of a goal. It took a few years and several attempts, but we finally settled on this one:

> **A GOAL IS SOMETHING SPECIFIC ONE WANTS TO ACHIEVE**
>
> **IT MUST BE IN WRITING**
>
> **IT MUST HAVE A DEADLINE**
>
> **IT MUST INCLUDE A PLAN**

John Goddard and his goals

As I indicated a few chapters back, it's always helpful to have a good story accompany your lesson. For teaching about goal-setting, there's no finer story than John Goddard. I first read about him in *LIFE* magazine in the early 1970s, at about the same time I started teaching about goals. Goddard was born in 1915 and grew up in the Los Angeles area. One of the things he heard constantly while growing up was the lamenting of the adults about what they *hadn't* done with their lives. "I wish I would have done this ... I wish I would have done that ..." and on and on and on.

By the time he was in high school, he decided that he'd heard enough. He was absolutely determined that life was not going to slip by him like it had all these adults. He made up his mind to learn as much as he could, and then lead a life of adventure and excitement. He didn't want to have to look back some day with regret and say, "I wish I would have ..." And he didn't **ever** want to be bored. On a rainy Sunday afternoon he sat down at the kitchen table and wrote 127 things he wanted to accomplish in life. Some of his goals had many parts to them, such as "Visit every country in the world," so the list actually contains almost 400 goals.

John Goddard achieved most of his goals and has led one of the most interesting and fulfilling lives of anyone I've ever known. We communicated frequently in the 1990s, and he was delighted that I was teaching about goal-setting. He said in a letter to me, "Every kid in the country should be learning about goal-setting every year they're in school." As I write this, he is 83 years young and going strong. Two of my great treasures are an autographed picture and autographed book about his trip down the full length (4,000 miles) of the Nile River.

I typed up Goddard's goals, made copies, and had my students look them over. The list generated some wonderful questions and discussion, and it helped fire up my students about writing their own goals. Goddard's list of goals can be found in the first edition of *Chicken Soup for the Soul*, compiled by Jack Canfield and Mark Victor Hansen, and published in 1993. But an even easier way to locate these goals is to visit Goddard's website: www.johngoddard.info/ life_list.htm. If all else fails, you can always "Google" John Goddard.

Teacher's have goals, too

To make the goal-setting unit more personal, I shared parts of my own story. I was very fortunate to have Sister Mary Anne as my eighth-grade teacher. Shortly before we graduated, she had us write 10 lifetime goals. She worked with us to make them real goals, not just vague wishes. She then gave them to our mothers with the instructions to give them back to us when we turned 21 or graduated from college. My Mom did give them back to me the year I graduated, and I've added hundreds of goals to the list since ever since. I usually add 20 every year on January 1.

I shared those original 10 goals with my students, which they found both interesting and funny. One of them was to earn $10,000 in one year. That was pretty good money back when I wrote it – maybe the equivalent of earning $100,000 today. They also wanted to know if I had achieved them all. My answer was no. I achieved eight of them and pointed out that if a person can achieve 80 percent of a lot of worthy goals, he or she will have a good life. In case you're curious, the two I didn't achieve pertained to basketball. One was to be an All-American player in college, and the other was to play in the NBA. Neither of those happened. I had the size, some athletic ability, a great attitude, and the right work ethic. Then why didn't I achieve those two goals? Notice I said I had "some" athletic ability. That means I didn't have the elite ability it takes to be an All-American and play in the NBA. In other words, I wasn't good enough.

But my students found that interesting also. And there's a lesson there – no one can achieve everything he or she wants. But it shouldn't stop us from going for it. Our efforts usually lead to something good. In this case, my basketball ability and efforts *did* lead to a "full ride" – an athletic scholarship that covered tuition, room and board, books, and fees. It also led to a passion for staying in shape, the opportunity to travel, healthy competition, and life-long friendships.

I didn't want to share all of my goals with my students because I thought it might appear as if I was bragging about what I had achieved in life. Instead, I shared with them my "Fun/Adventure" goals and told them I'd make the entire list available to anyone who wanted to see it during non-class time. A surprising number of them did. Here's a partial list of the goals I shared in class:

Fun/Adventure Goals

Go deep-sea fishing in the Florida Keys

Go salmon fishing in Alaska

Go parasailing in Hawaii

Ride a helicopter in NY City

Ride a helicopter in the Grand Canyon

Go heli-hiking in the Canadian Rockies

Visit the Basketball Hall of Fame

Visit the Baseball Hall of Fame

Visit the Football Hall of Fame

Visit the Negro Leagues Hall of Fame

Visit the Women's Hall of Fame

Snorkel in the Great Barrier Reef

Attend a Rolling Stones concert

See a play on Broadway in NY

See a show at Radio City Music Hall

Run the Boston Marathon

Visit the Artic Circle

Attend a Presidential inauguration

Ride in a hot air balloon in Africa

See Mt. Rushmore

Swim in the Mediterranean Sea

Go to the top of the Eiffel Tower

See Niagara Falls

Visit the Galapagos Islands

Cruise the Nile River

Visit the Sphinx and Great Pyramids

Visit all 50 states

Visit St. Peter's and the Sistine Chapel

Cross the English Channel

Watch a snake charmer in Morocco

Attend a World Series

Walk on the Great Wall of China

Visit Machu Pichu in Peru

Ride an elephant in Thailand

Go on a safari in Tanzania

Visit the Rock of Gibraltar

Ride the TGV train in France

Attend an MLB All-Star Game

Attend an NBA All-Star Game

See a show at Opryland

Drive across the United States

See the President's Oval Office

Visit the Rock n' Roll Hall of Fame

Attend an NCAA basketball Final Four

Go to the top of the St. Louis Arch

Own a red sports car

Take a lap around the Indianapolis 500

Play in the Softball World Series

Meet Willie Mays

Meet Harry Truman

See a game at Wrigley Field

See a game at Fenway Park

See a game at Yankee Stadium

See a game at Madison Square Garden

Attend an NBA Championship game

Go white-water rafting

Go cross-country skiing

See Sutherland Falls in New Zealand

Go to the top of the Empire State Bldg

Tour Venice by canal

I don't list these here to impress you, and I hope you don't interpret this as bragging. I shared them with my students for a couple of reasons. One, it was eye-opening to them that a teacher would want to do all of these things, and it generated all types of interest and questions. Too often our students think we're not normal people. Too often they think the principal locks us up at night in the workroom and lets us out the next morning. Too often they think all we do is correct papers and watch educational TV. We should reveal our fun side to them, and this was a way I could do it. Another reason I showed them these particular goals is that they reinforced John Goddard's message that one can have a life of fun and excitement if he or she plans for it.

How many of the above have I achieved? All but one. As I write this I have two more states to visit – Vermont and North Dakota. I plan on getting to both of them soon. I also suggest that teachers write their own goals. No matter what your age or your financial status, I guarantee that if you write down specific goals, put a deadline on them and develop a plan, you'll enrich your life. I'm so grateful for Sister Mary Anne and John Goddard because my goals, along with the right attitude, have led to a full and rewarding life. I'm in my 60s as I write this book, and I still write 20 yearly goals every January 1. My 20th goal for the year 2007 was to complete the first draft of this book by December 31. I made it – just barely.

After teaching my high school students about goal-setting for a few years, I started wondering if my adult students at the University of San Francisco had any goals, if they had ever been taught anything about goal-setting. I asked, and the answer was no to both questions. I gave them the same 10-goal assignment I'd given my high school students. They came back a week later, not only with their 10 goals, but also with an increased level of enthusiasm. Many of them were working in the high-stress, high-tech industry of Silicon Valley, and they said this assignment helped them get out of their ruts. It reminded them that there's a life out there besides work, and that it's full of opportunities and possibilities.

I was delighted that many of them made some life-changing decisions as a result of writing down their goals. One woman even quit her job and moved to Vienna, Austria, simply because it was something she had always wanted to do. Some of them wrote their goals with their spouses and started making plans to enrich their lives as a joint effort. I still hear from many of them, including the woman in Vienna.

Goal categories

After my students struggled with writing their first 10 goals, I gave them fair warning that the final assignment involved writing a hundred goals. Some thought I was kidding. I said, "Trust me, the 100 will be easier and more fun to write than the first 10." They weren't convinced. But after working on the next handout, they started to believe me. It was a sheet of paper with 16 categories of goals and space to write under each heading. Here's what I gave them:

Education	**Career**	**Family**	**Financial**
Personal growth	**Fun/adventure**	**Athletic**	**Own**
Travel (U.S.)	**Travel (world)**	**Learn to…**	**Events**
Read	**Accomplish**	**Service to others**	**Special interest**

Since it was a full sheet of paper, they had more space than presented here. We discussed the categories, and some students had questions. I also encouraged them to add any of their own categories they wanted. They also were allowed to skip categories. In less than 20 minutes, most of my students had written 50 or more goals. After this sheet came the final assignment, which is on the next page.

100 Goals

Please do this assignment in blue or black ink. It will be even better if you do it on a computer with a good printer. It is due at the beginning of the period on Tuesday, June 5.

Part 1 – Write at least 100 lifetime goals (You may write more if you wish)

Please divide them into categories. Choose your categories based on your interests. Use any of the categories I gave you earlier, ignore any you want, and write any new categories that work for you. Please number each goal.

Part 2 – Top Ten – After you write the 100 goals, select the 10 that are the most important to you. Write them in any order. Then select your number one goal and write a paragraph explaining why it is important to you.

You have two choices:

1 – Treat this as just another stupid school assignment that will earn you some grade points, or

2 – Treat it as if you're writing out a preliminary blueprint for the rest of your life. Think about some of the wild possibilities and write them down. Write out a life plan that will keep you from becoming one of those "nice dead people" who go through the motions of living, but never really live. Write out goals that will keep you from turning into Norma or Norman Nothing. Have fun.

PLEASE THINK IN TERMS OF POSSIBILITIES!

Advice from effective goal setters

1) Write down your goals in a special place.

2) Put deadlines on your big goals.

3) Write your goals in categories. Balance is important.

4) Include a category of self-improvement/personal growth.

5) Establish yearly goals from your main goal list.

6) Review/revise, add to your goals each January.

7) Look at your goal list on a regular basis (at least weekly).
    VERY IMPORTANT

8) Share your goals only with people who are likely to encourage you.

9) Think about your goals often. Picture yourself achieving them.
    VERY IMPORTANT

10) Decide what you're willing to give up in order to attain your goals. They don't come without some sacrifice.

11) Develop a plan for achieving your big goals.

12) Let your goals be a blueprint that can be changed, not a strait-jacket that keeps you bound.

13) Think big, challenge yourself, take risks, be willing to fail.

14) Always think in terms of **possibilities**, not limitations.
    MOST IMPORTANT

I always had fun teaching, but I had more fun teaching about goal-setting than any other subject. I'm not suggesting that you do all the same things I did. But I *am* suggesting that you help your students see the possibilities for their lives. I also hope you'll write some goals of your own. They really do make life better.

> *The purpose of goals is to focus our attention. The mind will not reach toward achievement until it has clear objectives. The magic begins when we set goals. It is then that the switch is turned on, the current begins to flow, and the power to accomplish becomes a reality.*
>
> *– Wynn Davis*

Good teachers catch kids doing things right

The most effective behavior management technique is the easiest to implement … "catching 'em being good." Research shows us that the quickest and most effective way to promote the display of appropriate behaviors is to reward them. We all like to have our efforts acknowledged, and will show more of that behavior if it brings us rewards. If only I could convince teachers to include this approach into their teaching style.

– Dr. Thomas McIntyre
State University of New York

An alternative to the "bad kid" notice

During my first year of teaching I was having some problems with a student who just couldn't seem to behave in class. He was negative, angry, disrespectful to me, and downright cruel to his classmates. I hadn't encountered anything like this during student-teaching, so I was inexperienced and ill-equipped to handle it as professionally as I would have liked. So I turned to one of my more experienced colleagues, a woman who had been teaching Social Studies for more than 20 years. After I explained the problem and gave her a few anecdotes, she responded with this advice: "I'd send a cinch notice home on the little bugger."

The look on her face and the tone of her voice led me to believe that she wasn't going to be a lot of help, but it sure made me curious as to what a "cinch notice" was. So I asked. She told me it was a district-wide form used by teachers when students behaved badly. She added, "There are thousands of them up in the workroom." I asked, "Is it really called a 'cinch notice?'" She said, "No, the district calls it a 'warning notice,' but we think 'cinch notice' describes it better, so that's what we've always called it." I was still a bit confused about the terminology, but not wanting to appear as a complete doofus to my colleague, I thanked her and let it go at that.

I went immediately to the nearest dictionary so I could look up the word "cinch." This is what it told me: "to tighten something by constricting it." A picture immediately popped into my head – my Social Studies colleague putting a noose around the neck of one of her students before slowly tightening it. That ought to fix the problem. That ought to straighten out the "little bugger." My next stop was the teacher's workroom so I could see the real thing. It listed at least 10 negative behaviors, including "bad attitude." There was a little box next to each, so all the teacher had to do was check each one that applied. Just in case all the negative behaviors weren't covered, there was additional space for writing in others. The form was in triplicate – one went home, one went to the vice-principal, and one stayed with the teacher. I just shook my head and wondered how sending one of these nasty little forms was going to result in better behavior.

A few days later I got the students' take on the whole thing. I started eating lunch in my classroom every day right after I discovered that the teachers' lounge was the most toxic place on campus. Since I was going to be there anyway, I told my students they could use the room at lunchtime for a variety of reasons – make up a missed test, do homework, eat lunch, socialize with their friends, sleep, whatever. I was delighted that so many of them took me up on my offer.

One day two kids came in during the lunch period to work on their math homework, which was due the next period. One of the students hadn't finished his assignment yet because he couldn't figure out how to solve two of the problems. His buddy was a math whiz and offered to help him. They politely assured me they weren't cheating. One was simply helping (teaching) the other. I was fine with that, so they sat down at desks that were pretty close to mine and went to work.

After the problems got solved, their conversation turned to other matters. One of them said, "Boy, I sure got yelled at last night. Mr. Gilmore sent a 'bad-kid notice' home on me and I got into all kinds of trouble." The other responded, "You're lucky you only got one. I got two 'bad-kid notices' on the same day – one from Mr. Gilmore (he must have sent a lot of them), and one from Mrs. Atkinson. My parents went nuts. I got grounded for the next two weekends." I wasn't eavesdropping, but I couldn't help hearing what they had said, and it was truly upsetting. It was bad enough that we had a "cinch notice." Did we have something even worse?

I looked over at these two genuinely nice kids and said, "*Please* tell me we don't really have something at this school called a 'bad-kid notice.'" They smiled, and one told me, "Oh, that's just our name for it. The teachers call it a 'cinch notice.'" Although I knew what was coming next, I still had to ask, "Why do you call it a 'bad-kid notice?'" The answer: "Because you only get 'em when you're a bad kid." Then I showed just how naïve and idealistic I was in that rookie year by asking, "What do teachers send home when you do something good?" They looked at me somewhat in disbelief. They might have been wondering what planet I was from, but they were too polite to ask. Their one-word answer was not a surprise: "Nothing."

The bell rang, the two students went on to their math class, and I went to the door to greet the students in my next class. I couldn't get the "bad-kid notice" out of my head, not only for the rest of that day, but for several days afterwards. It seemed strange that we had a form for recognizing negative behavior (and printed them up by the thousands) but had nothing for recognizing positive behavior. Maybe I *was* naïve and maybe I *was* idealistic, but common sense and logic told me we needed to acknowledge kids when they did good things. You may recall that I wrote in the early pages of this book that a teacher's primary responsibility is to bring out the best in his or her students. Catching kids doing things right is one of the most effective ways to do it.

A couple of days later I made an appointment with the principal so I could discuss the "warning/cinch notice" with him. I told him about the two boys who had been in my room at lunch a few days earlier and asked him if he was aware that the kids called it a "bad-kid notice." He smiled and said, "No, I wasn't aware of that, but it fits. If they do something they're not supposed to do, they get what they deserve." Then he asked, "Do you have a problem with our cinch notice? It's been used in the district since before you were born." I told him that I wasn't advocating the elimination of it, but suggested that we might want to have another form that balances things up, one that acknowledges kids when they do good things.

I could tell what was coming from the look on his face. He said, "That's not our job. Kids are *supposed* to behave appropriately. They don't deserve extra recognition for doing what's expected of them. Our job is to educate them, not to spoil and pamper them by telling them how wonderful they are all the time. That's not the way it is in the real world." He went on to tell me that I wasn't the first first-year teacher to come in with an idea that was going to change the world of education for the better. He said, "You're young and idealistic, and I appreciate that. But keep in mind that you're also a bit naïve. Wait until you've been around for a few years. You'll see things differently."

He also told me that the district office would never go for the idea of "wasting money" on positive notices. He said it would take too many hours to develop, it would be too expensive, and teachers wouldn't use them anyway. Then he added, "If you feel a need to do this on your own, I don't want to discourage you. You can acknowledge your own students if you want, but if you develop some kind of notice you'll have to pay for it yourself." I figured that would be no problem. After all, I *was* earning $8,400 in that first year of teaching.

Even though he left me on my own, I was determined to come up with something that would help me acknowledge my students in positive and affirming ways. This was way before personal computers, graphics programs, and laser printers, so I had to explore resources beyond the school district. I found out the name of the company that printed the district's flyers, newsletters, etc., and went to see how much it would cost to develop a "good-kid notice." Fortunately, the woman who waited on me was a kind soul and loved what I was doing. She even said, "All teachers should do this." She also knew that I was paying for it myself, promised to give me the district discount, and went the extra mile in helping me.

The school colors of San Carlos High School, where I did my first 16 years of teaching, were red and white. So we created a simple little notice on white glossy paper and did all of the printing in red. A copy of it is on the next page. Try to imagine the black lettering in vivid red.

GOOD KID NOTICE

STUDENT: _____

Subject: _____ Period: _____ Date: _____

Reasons for this notice:

_____

_____

_____

_____

San Carlos High School   _____

   Social Studies Dept.   Hal Urban

The exact size of the notice was 4 1/4 X 5 1/2 inches. In other words, it was a half sheet of paper. That way I could have two of them printed on one piece of paper, cut it in half, and convince myself that I was getting two for the price of one. I mailed them in regular school envelopes – with the principal's permission, of course.

I used this form from 1966–1982. It worked so well I never saw a need to change it, even though there had been incredible advances in technology. But when my beloved school was closed down due to declining enrollment, I moved to another school in our district, Woodside High School. A new school meant different colors – orange and black – so I needed a new Good Kid Notice. One of my colleagues, who was an expert on a program called PageMaker, did this one for me in about 10 minutes. Try to visualize it on orange paper.

GOOD KID NOTICE

STUDENT: _____

SUBJECT: _____ PERIOD: _____

Comments: _____
_____
_____

Woodside High School
Social Studies Dept.

Hal Urban

Date: _____

Responses to the Good Kid Notice

It would be the biggest understatement in this book if I said my simple little notice went over well. I was often amazed at how dramatically many of the parents and the kids responded. Apparently, this tiny bit of cheerful news filled a huge need. I'm not claiming that everyone responded this way, but enough of them did to let me know that I'd stumbled upon something that was far more meaningful than I'd originally thought. I could probably fill more than 300 pages with touching stories of how this small amount of positive recognition touched my students and their families.

I still have vivid memories of the first one I ever mailed to a home. It was for Scott, a senior taking American Government in his last semester of high school. Scott was what we might call an "average" kid. He wasn't really into school that much – he struggled to get C's, didn't play sports, wasn't in student government, and wasn't in drama or music. In other words, he didn't get a lot of recognition at school. There was something about Scott, however, that did stand out to me – his manners. He was one of the most polite, gracious, considerate, and friendly students I ever taught. I marveled at his ability to connect with both his classmates and me in such a genuinely warm manner. So when I got my first set of Good Kid Notices back from the printer, I sent one to his parents. I wrote something like this: "Just a brief note to let you know how much I enjoy and appreciate having Scott in my class. His manners and social skills are truly rare for a person his age. He seems to have a special knack for making other people feel good. Congratulations on raising such a fine young man. I look forward to meeting you at graduation."

A couple of days later I found a note in my mailbox that Scott's mother had called and requested that I call her back. I called at the end of the school day, and when she answered I said, "Hi, Mrs. Malloy, this is Hal Urban from San Carlos High. I'm returning your phone call." She said, "Oh, Mr. Urban ..." and then started crying. Somewhere in there she managed to eke out, "Please hold on a minute." After she gathered herself she said, "Mr. Urban, you'll never know how much that Good Kid Notice meant to Scott and how much it means to his father and me." She went on to tell me that it was the first time in his four years of high school that they had ever received anything positive from the school about their son. She said he had gotten his share of "cinch notices," and they simply never expected anything like this.

She also told me that she and her husband had been very diligent in teaching Scott and his younger brother the importance of good manners. They were proud of both their sons, but she often wondered if anyone else ever noticed. She said it "was so reaffirming" to know that their efforts were paying off. I assured her that Scott's social skills would pay huge dividends throughout his life, and that, in fact, I had learned a few valuable things from him. She cried again.

In case you're wondering what became of Scott, I want to complete the story. He wasn't into school because he knew exactly what he was going to do in life. He had some outstanding skills in woodworking, and he knew early that he was going to become a custom cabinetmaker as soon as he completed high school. He's been one for several years now, and the waiting list for his workmanship is a long one. He makes a lot of money, has a family, and is still as gracious as ever.

I have literally hundreds of other stories regarding the Good Kid Notice. And while I can't share all of them here, I do want to tell you one more that occurred in the spring of 2000, my next-to-last year in the classroom. Curtis was a senior in his last semester of high school, and decided to take my elective course in Psychology. He got off to about as bad a start as was possible. When I explained on the first day that the course was one in personal development, Curtis loudly and proudly proclaimed that he was "already fully developed." He and two of his buddies got a laugh out of his comment, but no one else did. He and his two friends proceeded to make fun of what I was doing, put down their classmates, act like tough guys, and be generally disruptive and obnoxious.

I rarely had to deal with this type of behavior, especially in an elective class such as Psychology. But there's no way it was going to continue past the first day. I discreetly asked each of them to stick around for a few minutes after class. They did, and I asked them why they had signed up for the class. The first one said his counselor put him in the class because she thought it would help him, but he thought "personal development was for pansies." The second one said he didn't know why he was in the class because he wanted to take Ceramics instead. Curtis said he really wanted to be in the class. I asked the first two if they had ever heard of St. Ignatius Loyola. Somehow it didn't surprise me that they hadn't. I told them that he had been one of the world's great educators, and among other things, he said, "No one learns until he's ready to learn." I suggested that if they didn't feel ready to learn about the psychology of personal growth and development, it was still early enough to get into another elective. They both got into Ceramics and Curtis stayed in Psychology.

The next day Curtis' mother called to tell me that he had shared the episode with her. She asked me if I knew who Curtis' sister was. I said yes. Even thought I hadn't taught her, I knew her by reputation – graduated with a 4.3 grade average, valedictorian of her class, perfect SAT score, and a full academic scholarship to Stanford. The mother said, "Curtis isn't anything like his sister." I knew that. She also told me, "Teachers constantly ask Curtis why he can't be more like his sister." That made me both sad and angry. Teachers should know better than that. I learned not to compare my students with their siblings when I was student-teaching.

She told me Curtis was gifted in other ways, especially in creating videos, but that he wasn't "academic," and he had always suffered due to comparisons with his sister. She said she was glad that he'd decided to stay in my class. I told her I was also. In fact, Curtis did very well in the class. Freed from the peer pressure of his two negative friends, he blossomed. This was a kid who really wanted to develop his potential and to become more mature, and he worked hard at it. He also worked on his social skills and became popular with his classmates. He had become the proverbial teacher's dream.

About six weeks later I decided it was time to acknowledge Curtis' progress and efforts. My Good Kid Notice to his parents said, "Curtis has come a long way since the first day – maybe one of the biggest and most positive changes I've ever seen in such a short time. He's polite, hard-working, and wants to learn. What more could a teacher ask for?" His mother called me again a few days later. She said Curtis cried when she showed it to him. He also told her that it meant more to him than the diploma he was going to receive in a few months. He knew the diploma was coming. He didn't think he'd ever receive any positive recognition from anyone at the school. By the way, Curtis is now a very successful video producer and recently got married.

Not all of my stories are this dramatic, but they're all touching. There are some parents (the ghost type) who don't respond at all, and that's OK. The most important thing is that a high percentage of these notices fill a human need for recognition and bring joy to a family. Sending home Good Kid Notices was one of my favorite things to do as a teacher.

A few suggestions regarding the Good Kid Notice

Here are some valuable tips I learned along the way while catching kids doing things right:

- If you put the notice in a school envelope, put your name on it near the address. Also write "GOOD NEWS!" somewhere on the envelope. Otherwise, kids will see that it's something from the school, assume the worst, and possibly even ditch it before their parents open it.

- Keep a record. After a while, I couldn't remember who'd already received a notice and who still deserved one. I made copies of my roll sheets, put them in a folder just for Good Kid Notices, and wrote the date down next to the name each time I sent one.

- Don't go overboard in making sure every student gets one. They should be earned. An insincere notice will do more harm than good. I tried hard to find something praiseworthy about each student, but it wasn't always possible.

- There are some other formats you can use: a post card, an e-mail, a phone call, a letter, or a completely different form.

- These are the reasons I sent notices: being considerate and polite, improvement in any area, good attitude, contributions to class discussions, hard work, helping a classmate, perfect attendance, sincere desire to learn, asking good questions, acts of kindness, consistency on homework, and anything else I could find that was genuine and worthy of recognition.

In summary, look for the good. After you find it, let the student and his or her parents know what you found. You might be sending home just the right words at just the right time. The student will feel good, the parents will feel good, and you'll feel good. You'll also be rewarding and reinforcing good behavior.

> *To say "well done" to any bit of good work is*
> *to take hold of the powers which have made the*
> *effort and strengthen them beyond our knowledge.*
>
> *– Phillips Brooks*

> *Give the other person a good reputation to live up to.*
>
> *– Dale Carnegie*

Good teachers get better every year

The best teachers enter the profession with a passion, as if there's a fire burning inside. And they learn early in their careers how to keep it burning. They fan the flame by always looking for new and better ways to reach their students and to more effectively present their material. That's why they get better year after year.

– Professor Erwin G. Hall

"How's teaching?"

You can probably imagine how many times I got asked the above question during my 35 years in the classroom. One person seemed to ask it more than anyone else. Her name is Ginger, and she was one of those "dream parents" back in the early 1990s when I taught her son Chase, who just happened to be one of those "dream students." Because Ginger and I lived in generally the same area and shopped at many of the same places, we frequently ran into each other. She would always ask me, "How's teaching?" And I would always tell her how good things were going. This went on for about 10 years.

The last time I saw Ginger was at a gas station in 2001. She asked her usual question, "How's teaching?" My exact words were, "This is the best year yet!" She smiled and said, "Oh, Hal, you say that every time I see you." Smiling back at her, I responded, "And every time I see you it's the truth. Teaching just continues to get better and better." She asked me why that was, especially since she'd been hearing that the schools were worse and the kids were harder to teach. I answered, "Maybe it's because I have more tricks up my sleeve now. After all these years in the classroom, I think I'm finally getting it down."

I probably heard Ginger's question – "How's teaching" – more than 500 times altogether, especially after passing the 20-year mark. My friends in other professions never quite understood how a person could be surrounded by kids all day, work such long hours, not make much money, and still love his job. When I told them I loved it more than ever, it confounded them even more. Another question I've been asked frequently since leaving the classroom is, "During your 35-year career, was there any one period that was the best to teach in?" My answer has always been, "Yes – the last 10." All the years were challenging, hard work, rewarding, and fun, but the last 10 really were the best. I think there were two reasons.

The first was that I discovered Tom Lickona's wonderful book, *Educating For Character: How Our Schools Can Teach Respect And Responsibility*, in the early 1990s. Reading it made me realize that I wasn't a voice in the wilderness. There were other educators out there who also believed we had a responsibility to help kids both increase in knowledge *and* develop good character. Tom's wonderful message affirmed what I'd been doing for years and bolstered my passion and enthusiasm for the stretch run of my career.

The second reason is that I made a commitment when I started teaching to improve every year, to never get complacent, to never burn out, and to walk out of my classroom on the last day knowing that I'd always given my best. I don't want to make myself out to be a hero, and I hope it doesn't come across as bragging, but I kept that commitment. It's a commitment that I would encourage every educator to make, no matter where you are in your career path. We get out of life what we put into it. We get out of teaching what we put into it. Like one of the signs in my classroom asked:

> # WHY NOT YOUR BEST?

A few words about "teacher burnout"

When I was in graduate school working toward obtaining my California Teaching Credential, I never heard the mention of "teacher burnout" by any of my professors. Maybe they didn't want to scare us off. But I heard the term many times in my first year of teaching, and unfortunately, every year afterwards. People spoke of it as if it was a disease, and I was warned repeatedly in my early years that it could strike me at any time. Some teachers admitted they had it, and others seemed to even brag about having it. Apparently it was an act of great courage on their part to continue coming to school each day while suffering from this dreaded disease.

Early in my first year, just before learning to stay out of the faculty lounge, another teacher, after hearing me wax excitedly about a recent lesson, commented, "Oh, yeah – the pep of the rookie teacher! We all had it once. Just wait until about year 15 or 20, and you'll get TB just like the rest of us." I naïvely asked, "Why would teachers get tuberculosis after that many years?" "Teacher burnout, my friend, teacher burnout," he said. "It happens to the best of us. The more energy you expend in the early years, the earlier it gets you." I assured him that it would never get me, to which he responded, "We'll see."

I never bought into the teacher burnout syndrome. I didn't then, I didn't during any of my years in the classroom, and I don't now. In addition, I've met literally thousands of other dedicated teachers and educators at all levels that seem to be immune from it. The reason is simple. Teacher burnout, like life burnout, is a choice. It starts with choosing a bad attitude – cynicism, which is the opposite of idealism. That cynicism often grows into full-blown negativity, and eventually it leads to the dreaded burnout.

Maybe some people discover early that they aren't suited for the teaching profession. Their best decision is to leave and find something that works better for them. It happens in all professions. But sticking around after one has burned out is a completely different story. That person harms the school, the students, and him or herself. I saw the devastating effects of it many times.

The best teachers not only have a passion for what they do, but they know how to keep it alive. They look for new and better ways to teach, and they renew themselves personally and professionally. In other words, they fan the flame.

The fifth choice – renewal

Back in Chapter 14, I explained the four most important choices we make other than faith. To refresh your memory and not make you turn back several pages, here are the choices that lead to genuine success in life: attitude, how we treat others, how hard we work, and how honest we are. Once we get through the rigors of college and graduate school and get established in our teaching careers, a fifth choice becomes critical. There are other names for it, but I call it renewal. Here are two definitions of it:

Restore to freshness, vigor; regenerate; to become new, or as new.
– Merriam-Webster Collegiate Dictionary

To develop skills, attitudes, habits of mind and the kind of knowledge and understanding that will be the instruments of continuous change and growth.

– John W. Gardner

Here are some wonderful "re" words that have similar meanings. As you look at them, please ask yourself if they apply to your life and to your career in education. If they do, you'll never burn out. You'll get better every year.

revive	rejuvenate	refresh
restore	reinvent	recharge
revitalize	reawaken	reinvigorate
recreate	regenerate	resurge
recapture	rediscover	redevelop

For those of you who are significantly younger than I am, you might not be familiar with John W. Gardner. Because he's one of my all-time heroes, and because he had a major impact on my teaching career, I want to tell you a little bit about him and his teachings on renewal. Gardner graduated from Stanford with high honors and went on to earn his Ph.D. at the University of California. After a couple of university teaching jobs, he joined the Marines during World War II. After the war he joined the Carnegie Corporation, and in 1955 he became the president of the Carnegie Foundation for the Advancement of Teaching.

I first became aware of him in the early 1960s while in college. John Kennedy, shortly after being elected President, appointed Gardner the Secretary of Health, Education and Welfare, a department that has since been divided into two. After Kennedy's death, Gardner founded Common Cause, an organization of citizens devoted to promoting open, honest, and accountable government. He's written several books, including *Excellence* and *Self-Renewal*, and at age 77 he became a professor of ethics at the Stanford Business School. He held that position until his death in 2002.

Shortly before he died I attended one of his last lectures at Stanford. It was about his favorite topic – renewal. Gardner was trained to be a teacher, started and ended his career as a teacher, and always said that it was both his first love and the most important profession in the world. He said that societies, organizations (including schools), and individuals either decay or renew themselves. He gave several examples throughout history. He said one of the most frightening things is that so many people, particularly those in mid-career, run out of steam. When they do that and don't figure out a way to renew themselves, they begin to decay.

He said, "We can't write off the danger of complacency, growing rigidity, and imprisonment by our own comfortable habits and opinions." He said it was scary to realize how many young people allow themselves to get trapped in "fixed attitudes and habits." He said the solution, no matter what our age or what our profession, is to regularly refresh and revitalize ourselves. That was the theme of Gardner's *Self-Renewal*, which was first published in 1963. I'd read it just before starting my teaching career, and it had an enormous influence on me. How wonderful it was to hear this great man reaffirm the truth of that book almost 40 years after it was written. Here was an 89-year-old man telling a large audience of people considerably younger than he was that renewal was central to a rewarding life or profession.

Suggestions for teachers who want to stay fresh

The seventh habit in Stephen Covey's great book, *The 7 Habits of Highly Effective People,* is "Sharpen the saw." What does that mean? It means the same thing as John Gardner's advice to renew ourselves. The opposite of sharp is dull, something no teacher wants to be. I discovered several ways to renew myself regularly as a teacher. Let me end this by sharing them with you:

- **Books on education and teaching** – There's a treasure trove of good books out there about our profession – more than there ever have been. Some of them are listed in the bibliography, but there are countless others available. In addition, there are new ones coming out each year. Few things are more helpful than reading about the successes of teachers and schools throughout the country.

- **The Internet** – This wasn't available to me during the first part of my career, but for people in the profession today it's an invaluable and seemingly limitless supply of helpful information. All you have to do is go to Google and type in key words like "Character Education," "best teachers," "successful schools," etc.

- **Conferences** – I went to my first educational conference during my second year of teaching. It was so valuable I continued to attend them through my last year in the classroom. You have the opportunity to learn new philosophies and strategies from experts in the field and from other teachers. You'll go away with new ideas and a new spirit.

- **Colleagues** – When I was a student-teacher at Washington High School in San Francisco, I had two excellent master teachers. I learned a great deal from observing them in the Fall semester before taking over their classes in the Spring semester. Although they were both excellent, I wanted to observe a greater variety of teaching styles. My students told me who the best teachers in the school were, I observed them, and picked their brains afterwards. These were invaluable experiences for a young person getting ready to enter the profession.

But the practice didn't end with my student teaching. During my first year of official teaching, I again asked my students who the best teachers were. Believe me, they know. It was no surprise that the same names came up over and over. I observed at least six of them and followed up by having long discussions with them. The best teachers are always willing to share what they've learned to help a colleague, especially a young one. I continued this practice even after becoming a veteran teacher, often observing teachers who were much younger, but who had some wonderful new ideas and strategies. It was my good fortune to be surrounded by many talented and committed educators during my career, and I took full advantage of it. I urge you to do the same.

- **Staff development days** – I'll be honest. I sat through quite a few stinkers during my 35 years of teaching. Our district had a penchant for bringing in speakers who were often both boring and insulting. I often wished I was teaching instead of listening to some outside consultant who was full of theories but clueless as to what life is really like in the classroom. But every once in a while the district would surprise us. Some of the experts they brought in had information of great value, and they made significant contributions to our school and to individual teachers. Of course, the best ones had been teachers themselves, and they managed to be entertaining, enlightening, and challenging.

- **Experimentation, trial-and-error** – I played it pretty safe during my first year of teaching. I had to because it was so overwhelming – making up lesson plans, learning how to manage five classrooms a day, dealing with discipline problems, correcting tests and papers, keeping records, attending meetings, returning phone calls, etc. It's a wonder any teacher survives the first year. But things got considerably more comfortable in the second year, and I kept thinking about what the good teachers had told me: "Don't be afraid to experiment." They all assured me that they'd fallen flat on their faces from time to time, but finding out what *didn't* work usually led to the discovery of what *did* work.

I can assure you that I had my share of flops, especially in those early years, but I learned. We stay fresh in the teaching profession by using our imaginations, by looking for new methods, by trying out new strategies, and by discovering new ways to make things work more effectively in the classroom. Keep what works well, but continue tweaking and looking for better ways. You'll never have to worry about burnout.

• **Your students** – Never underestimate how much you can learn from your students about good teaching. Students at all grade levels have always known more than teachers do about what works and what doesn't – and they've always been more than willing to tell us. Remember that they're the ones who sit in our classes every day; they're the ones who put up with us. It's important that we give them the opportunity to let us know how we're doing. We need to listen to them just as business leaders need to listen to their customers and their employees. Here's the most effective "teacher evaluation form" ever devised:

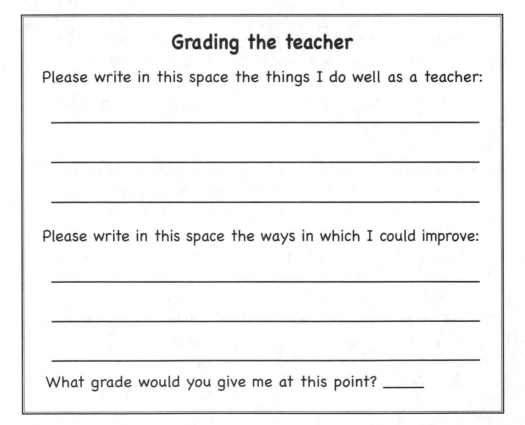

Grading the teacher

Please write in this space the things I do well as a teacher:

_____

_____

_____

Please write in this space the ways in which I could improve:

_____

_____

_____

What grade would you give me at this point? _____

A great teacher's advice

In his last speech to teachers, John W. Gardner told his audience that the average human being operates well below the level of his or her potential. He said our number one mission should be to help our students discover their potential for productive and rewarding lives. While we're doing this, we also need to increase our awareness of the undeveloped potential within ourselves. We need to continue learning and improving as individuals and as educators. He said, "I took on a new teaching job at age 77, and I'm still learning, still trying to get better every year." I hope you'll do the same.

The best teachers always aim for perfection, but never expect it. That's the reason they keep getting better.

– Marvin Berkowitz

Two wishes for teachers

Writing has always been an agonizing process for this author. But working on this book has been different. It was still hard and slow work, but far more enjoyable to write because it so often brought back memories of the many wonderful years I spent in the classroom. I also think working on this book was more enjoyable because each time I sat down at my computer I knew I was writing to the most important people in the world – teachers.

I want to leave you with two heartfelt wishes. The first is that the ideas I've shared here will help you become a better teacher. The second is that you find teaching to be as joyful and rewarding as I did. God bless you for what you do.

There's no word in the language that I revere more than "teacher." My heart sings when a kid refers to me as his teacher, and it always has. I've honored myself and the entire family of man by becoming a teacher.

– Pat Conroy
Prince of Tides

Teachers are expected to reach unattainable goals with inadequate tools. The miracle is that at times they accomplish this impossible task.

– Haim Ginott

In a completely rational society, the best of us would be teachers and the rest of us would have to settle for something else.

— Lee Iacocca

Teachers are, more than any other class, the guardians of civilization.

— Bertrand Russell

Teachers, I believe, are the most responsible and important members of society because their professional efforts affect the fate of the earth.

— Helen Caldicott, M.D.

Only a teacher? Thank God I have a calling to the greatest profession of all!

— Ivan Welton Fitzwater

Whoever first coined the phrase "you're the wind beneath my wings" most assuredly was reflecting on the sublime influence of a very special teacher.

— Frank Trujillo

Most of the significant advances in civilization have been the result of the work of teachers.

— James Marran

Books about teaching, schools, and character education

*All that mankind has done, thought, gained, or been, it is
lying as in magic preservation in the pages of books. They are
the chosen possession of men.*

— *Thomas Carlyle*

Educating for Character (How Our Schools Can Teach Respect and Responsibility) by Thomas Lickona. The flagship book of the Character Education movement.

Character Matters (How to Help Our Children Develop Good Judgment, Integrity, and Other Essential Virtues) by Thomas Lickona. An update on the flagship book with hundreds of stories about what works.

Smart & Good High Schools (Integrating Excellence and Ethics for Success in School, Work, and Beyond) by Thomas Lickona and Matthew Davidson. A must for any high school educator.

Schools Without Failure by William Glasser. The oldest book (1969) on the list, but still relevant and still full of excellent suggestions.

Marva Collins' Way by Marva Collins and Civia Tamarkin. The second oldest book (1982) on the list by a great "tough love" teacher.

Growing Character (99 Strategies for the Elementary Classroom) by Deb Austin Brown. A must for elementary educators. Creative lessons by an award-winning teacher.

The First Days of School by Harry Wong and Rosemary Wong. A classic which has sold more than 3 million copies. Written by two former teachers.

Restoring School Civility (Creating a Caring, Responsible, and Productive School) by Philip Fitch Vincent with David Wangaard and Paul Weimer. An update of ***Rules and Procedures*** which lives up to its title.

Developing Character in Students – A Primer by Philip Fitch Vincent. A treasure trove of the "basics" for helping kids develop good character. Written by an award-winning Character Education leader.

Life's Greatest Lessons (20 Things That Matter) by Hal Urban. Originally titled ***20 Things I Want My Kids to Know***, it's been used by teachers with students at all grade levels. It explains how life works in the real world and what's essential.

Positive Words, Powerful Results (Simple Ways to Honor, Affirm, and Celebrate Life) by Hal Urban. A reminder for both students and teachers about the powerful impact our words can have.

Character Education Organizations

Center for the 4th & 5th R's
Education Department
SUNY Cortland
P.O. Box 2000
Cortland, NY 13045
607/478-5684

Character Education Partnership
918 16th Street NW, Suite 105
Washington, DC 20006
800/988-8081

Cooperating School Districts/
Character Plus
1460 Craig Road
St. Louis, MO 63146
314/872-8282

Center for Youth Issues
6101 Preservation Drive
Chattanooga, TN 37416
800/477-8277

International Center for
Character Education
University of San Diego
5998 Alcala Park
San Diego, CA 92110
619/260-5980

Center for the Advancement
of Ethics and Character
Boston University
621 Commonwealth Avenue
Boston. MA 02215
617/353-4794

Developmental Studies Center
2000 Embarcadero, Suite 305
Oakland, CA 94606
510/533-0213

Center for Character
and Citizenship
University of Missouri-St. Louis
One University Blvd.
St. Louis, MO 63121
314/516-7521

The Giraffe Project
P.O. Box 759
Langley, WA 98260
360/221-7989

Institute for Global Ethics
11 Main Street
P.O. Box 563
Camden, ME 04843
207/236-6658

Character Counts
9841 Airport Blvd., Suite 300
Los Angeles, CA 90045
800/711-2670

Community of Caring
Eunice Kennedy Shriver Center
University of Utah
1901 E. South Campus Dr. #1120
Salt Lake City, UT 84112
801/587-8990

Positive Coaching Alliance
Athletic Department
Stanford University
Stanford, CA 94305
866/725-0024

School for Ethical Education
440 Wheelers Farms Road
Milford, CT 06460
203/783-4439

Thank You

Although the author usually gets most of the credit, there are always other people who play a critical role in producing a book. In this case there were eight people who contributed in different, but in equally important ways. My heartfelt appreciation for each of them goes far beyond the words written here.

Cathy Urban – All authors need support, patience, and a little sympathy from their significant others. I received all of these and more from my wife Cathy from beginning to end during the writing of this book. In addition to helping with the initial editing and making valuable suggestions, she was always understanding when I didn't come out of my cave for extended periods. For this I'm deeply grateful.

Karen Saunders and Kerrie Lian – After the writing and editing is complete, two critically important tasks remain in producing the finished product: interior design and layout for the printer, and creation of the front and back covers. It was my good fortune to work with Karen and Kerrie at MacGraphics on these two tasks. I'm in awe of both their talent and professionalism, and equally appreciative of how pleasant they were to work with.

Tom Lickona – I met Tom in the early 1990s when the Character Education movement was getting started. Since that time he's contributed mightily to both my speaking and my writing efforts, particularly in regard to this book. Every author should have a friend like him – one who's always there with just the right amounts of wisdom, support, and prayer.

Phil Vincent – One of the most influential leaders in the Character Education movement, Phil is also one of the busiest – as a speaker, writer, publisher, and consultant. But friends make time for friends, and when I needed him, he was always there with practical advice, encouragement, and humor. I thank him for his insight, and more importantly, for his friendship.

Michele Borba – Somewhere among her national and international speaking trips, her many appearances on the "Today Show," the answering of hundreds of e-mails on her Blackberry, and the writing of her own many books, Michele also made time for a friend. She has a special way of infusing others with her abundance of positive energy, and this author is deeply appreciative of her time, support, and friendship.

Marvin Berkowitz – Another one of the great leaders in Character Education, Marvin planted the first seeds that grew into this book. In a uniquely humorous and loving way, he suggested that I get all my teaching strategies down in writing before I go senile and forget them. And once I started writing, he was there every step of the way with both inspiration and practical suggestions. I'm honored to dedicate this book to him and to have him as a friend.

About The Author

Hal Urban earned bachelor's and master's degrees in history and a doctorate in education at the University of San Francisco. He did post-doctoral study in the psychology of peak performance at Stanford University.

Dr. Urban has often been described as a "teacher's teacher." He was an award-winning teacher at San Carlos High School (16 years), Woodside High School (19 years) and at the University of San Francisco (part-time for 36 years). Since 1995 he's been teaching teachers at all grade levels throughout the United States and in several foreign countries. He speaks at conferences and at schools, addressing educators, students of all ages, and parents.

At San Carlos High School he was presented with both the Distinguished Teacher Award and the Students' Choice Award. At Woodside High School he was selected Teacher of the Year twice by students and a third time by the administration. He was a Mentor Teacher five times in his school district. The students at the University of San Francisco honored him with both the Life-Long Learning Award and the Most Supportive Professor Award. In 1999 the Character Center presented him with the National Educator of the Year Award, and in 2005 the Character Education Partnership bestowed on him the Sanford N. McDonnell Lifetime Achievement Award.

His first book, *Life's Greatest Lessons*, was selected in 2000 by *Writer's Digest* as the Inspirational Book of the Year, and has sold more than 350,000 copies.

Website: www.halurban.com

E-mail: halurban@halurban.com

Phone: 650/366-0882

Books by Hal Urban

LIFE'S GREATEST LESSONS
20 Things That Matter

Simon & Schuster, 2003

POSITIVE WORDS POWERFUL RESULTS
Simple Ways to Honor, Affirm, and Celebrate Life

Simon & Schuster, 2004

CHOICES THAT CHANGE LIVES
15 Ways to Find More Purpose, Meaning, and Joy

Simon & Schuster, 2006

THE 10 COMMANDMENTS OF COMMON SENSE
Wisdom from the Scriptures for People of All Beliefs

Simon & Schuster, 2007

The above books are available from the author and anywhere books are sold

---

LESSONS FROM THE CLASSROOM
20 Things Good Teachers Do

Great Lessons Press, 2008

20 GIFTS OF LIFE
Bringing Out the Best in Our Kids, Grandkids, and Others We Care About

Great Lessons Press, 2012

Signed copies of these two books can be purchased directly from the author.

They're also on Amazon.com, but at a higher price.

Please see the next page for ordering instructions

ORDERING INFORMATION

These two books are not in bookstores. Save yourself a trip.

They *are* on Amazon, but cost more. Save yourself some money.

Buy directly from the publisher. Good prices and quick same-day service.

LESSONS FROM THE CLASSROOM:
20 Things Good Teachers Do
20.00

20 GIFTS OF LIFE:
Bringing Out the Best in Our Kids,
Grandkids, and Others We Care About
17.00

Postage/shipping: Prices vary, depending on the order and number of books. U.S. Postal Service is used for small orders (1-10). Fed Ex Ground is used for large orders (11+). Call or e-mail for rates. There are no handling fees added.

Bulk order discounts: Orders of 20, 50, 100, 150, 200 receive discounts. The more you buy, the cheaper they are. Call or e-mail for rates. Still no handling fees on large orders.

California residents: Add 8.50% sales tax to the book total.

Forms of payment: Check, money order, cash, purchase order, credit card, debit card.

Hal Urban
Great Lessons Press
790 Barbour Drive, Redwood City, CA 94062
Ph 650/366-0882 Fx 650/366-9882
E-mail halurban@halurban.com

Order directly from here:
www.halurban.com